"Have never read nor come close to the thoughts or suffering of someone who is so aware of his differences and diagnosis. A book that should be read by all in the health profession and by the families who love and struggle..."

- Ellen Riojas Clark, Ph.D., Professor Emerita
University of Texas at San Antonio

....

"What do you do when the systems of care struggle to provide effective support for loved ones suffering with persistent mental illness and co-morbid ailments? You share your heartbreak, expose your truths and advocate for change. Fran Wishnick has done that."

-Suzanne Jordan, Former President,
Mental Health Association, Ulster County, NY

....

"There are obvious lessons in Craig's life and death-- lessons that in most cases are still yet to be applied. But the more striking and more difficult problem is that we do not have "care" "systems" that are generally capable of responding to people whose needs (and strengths) are great but whose limitations fail to fit into prescribed categories."

-Michael Hogan, Ph.D., Chairman of President's
New Freedom Commission on Mental Health 2002-2003
Former State Mental Health Commissioner in CT, OH and NY

....

"Like a punch in the stomach. Beautifully written and seriously impactful. The avenging mother bear has the strength to move mountains."

-Nancy Cohen, Retired Executive

"It is clear that Craig tried so hard. It is also clear that our current systems do not understand or address the needs of a person like Craig."

-Robin Taliaferro, Educator

....

"I'm struck by Craig's e-mails. They give us such a vivid sense of him – both his so sincere and unwavering drive to experience and understand the world, a real wisdom, sensitivity and ability to self-reflect (unique at any age) and his pain, frustration and maybe shame..."

-Marsha Lazarus, Director of Workforce Development
Mental Health Association in New York State

....

"Craig Climbed a Tree provides unique insight into the mind of an individual suffering with mental illness and the siloed system that failed to help him despite his deepest desires. Reading Craig's own words was simultaneously heartbreaking and heartwarming."

-Lindsay Miller, Executive Director, New York Association on Independent Living

....

"This is such a painful and yet beautiful story. It has a lot to teach. I am especially moved by the clear evidence that the silos in our care systems and exclusionary criteria in helping systems in don't work for people. My heart breaks, but resolve strengthens."

-Susan Dooha, Executive Director, Center for Independence of the Disabled, New York

Craig Climbed A Tree

Fran & Craig Wishnick

FOREWORD

Reading of Craig Wishnick's struggle to understand this world and find a place where he could be comfortable in it is heartbreaking. Reading of his parents' efforts to help and the toll it took on their family is frustrating. Reading of the inability of the health care system to deliver appropriate solutions and treatments is enraging.

But read we must. Because there are too many Craig's in our country today and it is way past time we move beyond labels and diagnoses. We must discover what it takes to engage one-on-one with every person who suffers as Craig did; to help them feel healthy and whole. To help them find a place where they feel they belong.

In writing Craig's story, Fran Wishnick has let us hear his voice, as she and Ken so often heard it. And in letting us hear Craig, she gives voice to hundreds of thousands of others who struggle with chronic mental and physical illness. She highlights so many milestones and crossroads in his life where *"What if..."* questions are inevitable. In so doing, she makes one think of all the roads that were not taken; all the options that were not tried.

I never knew Craig. But I have known his despair and shared to pain of others longing to be understood. I've grasped for elusive solutions for young people I've raised, taught and mentored, just as Fran and Ken Wishnick did.

iv

But I never heard the voices of the mentally ill as clearly as I can hear Craig's voice now. The specificity of his questions; the articulation of thoughts and feelings in his head and heart provide rare insight. Though I didn't know him then, I can hear Craig now. His voice calls me to listen more intently to people who suffer as he did.

It's easy to become angry and cynical. But Craig's story, difficult as it is, invites a different conclusion. His story shines such a bright spotlight on the problems, that finding the solutions becomes more compelling. And that bright light makes things so much clearer that solutions start to seem possible again.

Joan Lawrence-Bauer
Reporter/Columnist
Catskill Mountain News

Table of Contents

Table of Contents

INTRODUCTION

It was a gorgeous summer day. Our family was in our front yard and our daughter and her friend had just climbed a small tree and run off. Our son Craig, 5 years old, wanted to climb also but couldn't figure out how. "Put your right foot there...good!" my husband Ken explained. Walking closer to the tree, Ken then methodically showed him where to put his hands and other foot as Craig climbed.

We have this picture of Craig smiling, feeling accomplished, happy that he got to that spot on the tree. We never imagined how difficult life would be for him, later.

Craig struggled with every cell of his being, but he was plagued with social anxiety, communication and language problems, black and white thinking, repetitive thoughts, inner turmoil and depression. He was constitutionally incapable of surviving in a world he could not understand or fix.

He never gave up on wanting help, but never quite believed he could be helped – a vicious cycle.

I am Craig's mom. Craig and I will tell his story together, through his e-mails and other writings I've saved.

Our book is for educators, therapists, policy-makers, families, and anyone who wants to gain a more intimate understanding of how a young person with enormous strengths and deficits tried to survive, but ultimately couldn't. It is my fervent hope that by delving into his story we can improve our systems of care, and the ways that we respond to each other.

I have changed the names of most people and places. Family member names have remained the same.

Chapter One: Eggie

I've been struggling with beginning this book. I write it to remember him, to honor him and, I hope, to help others. I'm not a writer. I'm a mom who has lost her son and who needs to tell his story. As I begin, it's now three months since his death. Despite his almost lifelong suicidal thoughts and expressions, it remains unbelievably shattering that he is gone.

During his life, Craig wrote extensively by e-mail and otherwise. His questions and insights reflected the struggles he had in understanding and accepting society, social norms, and how or whether he could ever fit in. Chronic depression was poignantly described, sometimes in vivid terms that are difficult to read and ponder. Nonetheless, his writings and questions articulate the thoughts of an intelligent, unique, and troubled mind. This book includes the e-mails and writings that we saved. I wish we had saved them all.

Fran and Craig Wishnick

I find it especially difficult to describe Craig in his early years. Born in 1983, our second child entered the world at Pennsylvania Hospital as a footling breech baby, via c- section. He was a beautiful, smiling baby who was welcomed into our New Jersey farmhouse by his two-year-old sister Lindsay, dad Ken, and me. Craig was an easy-going and charming baby—Lindsay called him "Eggie"— and met all the developmental milestones. He learned to walk at eleven months while being cared for by his grandparents (we were on vacation).

When he was still crawling—he was an extremely fast and comical crawler—he passed a blockade in our house and tried climbing up the steps. He was too quick and fell backwards as I was running over. He did not have a diagnosed concussion, but to this day we wonder, and I sometimes perseverate about, whether something neurological happened which adversely affected his brain for the rest of his life.

At around eighteen months of age, we began to see major differences between our daughter and our son. Craig would only play with one or two toys and completely disregard the rest. The play was often repetitive—for example, he would sit in one of the children's toy cars and put a key in and out. He often seemed bored. He cried if we picked him up or hugged him when he couldn't see us – he couldn't tolerate the surprising pick-up, and it clearly wasn't fun for him. He seemed especially sensitive to touch, noises and smells. When we tried to arrange play-dates with other children, he clung to me.

You know the saying, "Every child is different?" At first, we thought that we were just seeing normal differences. Soon we saw that wasn't the case.

When Craig turned two, we moved to Maryland. He had a difficult time with this transition, as he did subsequently with all changes in his life. He became oppositional, but we hoped it was just the "terrible twos." His speech was difficult to understand to everyone but me, since I was with him all the time. Wherever he was in the house, he thought he could just start talking to us. When presented with certain voice tones, sounds, or things he didn't want to hear, he would cover his ears. This included times when we were trying to give him information that he needed to know. Sometimes we got angry at him for not listening.

As soon as Craig became fully toilet-trained at two and-a-half, we enrolled him in pre-school, thinking he needed more experiences with other children, and more structure. I remember worrying when I watched him. He just didn't seem to be having fun. He generally watched other children and stayed outside the circle.

I saved a hand-written report by his pre-school teacher.

"Craig has always been quite aware and interested in what was taking place in the classroom and often looked as if he wanted to participate. However, for reasons unknown, Craig has been experiencing a difficult time interacting independently without the assistance of an adult."

In another nursery school, where I volunteered when Craig was four, his teacher observed he was:

"inattentive, easily distracted, demands must be met immediately, easily frustrated." "Craig seems to be academically on par although he doesn't readily share his thoughts or feelings so it is hard to evaluate him."

Our family became focused on Craig and his needs. From early morning on, Craig was "ready to go." In our town, there was a wonderful indoor pool with a twisty slide called a splashdown. On many mornings, I'd take Craig and Lindsay there and within an hour, he'd be done. We'd try different techniques to get him to entertain himself but none worked. He also tended to interrupt Lindsay's play with us and with her friends. We sent Craig to time-out frequently but it did not result in changes.

Usually, Craig would come back smiling but do a different version of the same behavior. We tried talking it through, giving him rewards and, alternatively, being tough. Eventually, we tried therapy with several different therapists but he didn't modify how he acted.

Craig's difficulties also influenced our family dynamics because we decided that I couldn't return to work until and unless we got Craig's situation under better control. (I had previously been a city planner.) Most families with a stay-at-home parent returning to work know there'll be some adjustment time with child-care, but also believe their child will eventually thrive. Given Craig's unusual behavior, difficulties with relationships and transitions, as well as language problems, we felt a responsibility to be with him until he could adjust. That plan lasted for 19 years.

When Craig entered kindergarten, he had already taught himself to read. The teachers in early elementary school were truly wonderful and connected with each child. Craig memorized the rules and often reminded teachers when they deviated from them. He did quite well in kindergarten and throughout elementary school, academically—except there were certain things he just didn't understand. At first, Craig didn't understand humor, and chose to study it. He wanted and demanded explanations of why things were funny, even on television. For example, when he first saw "Home Alone", he didn't grasp the jokes, and wanted to know why people were laughing. It was hard and sometimes felt impossible for us to explain, but Craig persisted. He would ask us or his teacher questions again and again until he got an explanation that satisfied him. He watched "Home Alone" many times, even as an adult.

In kindergarten, the students put on a show about the history of the United States, and Craig was a Civil War soldier. The teacher and parent volunteers all told the kindergarteners to be sure to speak especially loudly since it was a big auditorium and there would be lots of people. When it was his turn, Craig walked up to the microphone and screamed into it. Children and adults covered their ears. Craig had taken the instructions literally.

Craig had trouble figuring out things that weren't sequential, for example, movies or books that began at the end and went back and forth. He had difficulty recognizing family relationships beyond mother, father, brother, sister and grandparents. From time to time we tried to describe our own family relationships, such as cousins, aunts, and uncles, but for some reason, he simply didn't get it. I never understood why. Also, he had more difficulty than would be expected in distinguishing men from women, or girls from boys, if haircuts or dress were genderless.

Reluctantly, the school system agreed to do some testing when Craig was in first grade. The reluctance was because he got excellent grades, and school systems are usually hesitant to order testing unless they have to. Craig didn't have an easy time being pulled out of class to take tests. The examiner wrote that during one testing situation, "Craig talked throughout the sessions and asked many questions about the test, the examiner, the room, etc." Craig's results showed average intellectual functioning with some fine motor coordination difficulties, a moderate language disorder in the areas of language content, structure and auditory processing. One test administered to Craig was called Kaufman IQ. It revealed an unusually high separation of scores for sequential processing over simultaneous processing. Although those terms were new to us, Craig's strength in sequential processing and serious weaknesses in simultaneous processing made sense. He didn't have any problems following literal directions in step-by-step order. Yet, he was frustrated with simultaneous tasks such as puzzles where experimentation was key to success. For example, if Lindsay made a castle and handed Craig a pile of blocks, he had no idea how to begin building the whole.

For us, his low test scores in simultaneous processing also provided clues about why he had great difficulties with movies or books where the story wasn't told in a linear fashion.

As part of the testing, another aspect of Craig's mind was demonstrated when Craig was shown a picture of Abraham Lincoln and asked who he was. Instead of saying Lincoln was President, Craig said he was the man on the $5 bill! Craig continued to be very interested in money throughout his life, to the point of obsession.

As the stay-at-home parent, it was my task to advocate for Craig in the school setting. Often, teachers didn't accept the inconsistency between the excellent academic work that Craig could produce and the things he didn't understand. There were certain assignments that he needed to be excused from because he just couldn't do them. What choice did we have? I'm a strong advocate and got substitute assignments for him, but as the years went by, often teachers implied that Craig was choosing not to do assignments that he was, in fact, able to do. It was so confusing, especially for us. We never knew if we were doing the right thing by him. We questioned ourselves.

Craig was in regular classes, with pullout for speech and language services. On December 20, 2009, as an adult, Craig e-mailed about one of his childhood experiences with a speech and language matter. It's amazing and instructive to me that the twenty-five-year-old Craig was still processing lessons he learned when he was eight or nine:

I just started thinking recently back to my special education assistance I received in elementary school to help me with pronunciation of words and also taking things literally. Here's something pretty funny. One thing that the educator tried to do to help me was to read Amelia Bedelia where Amelia takes things too literally and does exactly as she is told. It's meant to be humorous, but when the educator helped me understand why it was supposed to be funny, I was almost psychoanalyzing Amelia Bedelia and wondering if the educator was reading this to me because she wanted me to become more like Amelia Bedelia!!! But I also sensed that she was making fun of Amelia, so that made me even more confused – LOL. I didn't realize she was explaining things to me because I needed to develop more of an understanding of multiple meanings of words, although unconsciously I think the educator might have helped for that to become a strength of mine at a relatively early age, even if I didn't appreciate the full humor but just knew it was funny for others. Now I love playing around with multiple meanings of words, as I think a lot of Aspies (Aspies is a shortened name that some young people with

Asperger's Syndrome have given themselves) do who are trying to grow and understand the neuro-typical world, even if sometimes just from a distance, because humor about our language and the world helps a bit in becoming more accepting of ourselves."

Out of boredom—or simply his hyper-need to structure his time—Craig asked for a blackboard in his room where he could write his plans for the day. Those plans were down to small intervals, sometimes 15 minutes. For example, he would ask us, "When are we going to do X?" and wanted a time. If we got a phone call or just weren't ready at that time, he got upset. It was actually more than upset. Years later, he was able to tell us that every time we told him something that turned out to be inconsistent, he considered that a lie and stored it in his memory. He was angry at us for these "lies" and was only able to explain that to us when he was about 25 years old.

Even as a youngster, Craig was extremely literal in his understandings and viewpoints. An example we remember well was when Craig came home from school one day very upset and told us one of his classmates had spit in the stream near our house. He called that "pollution" and said it would kill the fish and frogs.

Explanations didn't work – to him, spitting vs. pouring oil were equal in his black-and-white thinking.

Hand-eye coordination was definitely a strength for Craig. He played ping-pong, tennis and baseball exceptionally well. However, when we encouraged Craig to join teams to be part of something, anything, it never worked. Craig couldn't understand the social dynamics, and often responded inappropriately. Other kids (and adults) withdrew from him after getting unusual responses. I remember encouraging him to try baseball, soccer, tennis, after-school groups and cub scouts – he ended up leaving all.

When Craig was ten years old, he wrote, "If I Could Fly."

If I could fly, I would go straight up and maybe go on top of earth and fly to a planet. I would first go to Venus, then Mercury, then Mars, Jupiter, Saturn, Uranus, Neptune, then Pluto. I would fly back to Mars and go on the planet to see if there is life. If there was I would pick up stuff and bring it back to Earth and study it. Then I could tell people there was life on Mars. Next, I would probably carry another person to planets to earn money. By then I would probably be wealthy.

Socially, he tried to engage with neighborhood kids. Once, some parents came over to tell us that Craig had been hanging out in their backyard on their swing set without their children. He needed to stop doing that. Sometimes he would be invited to another child's house, but that didn't last long. He was never able to have or do sleepovers, and so he missed that normal childhood experience as well.

Then there was depression. In early elementary school, I clearly remember Craig asking us why people have to live if they don't want to. To us, this was a troubling, dark, and unanswerable question—and foreshadowed a lifetime of depression and suicidal ideation although it didn't become clear until his mid-teens. Meanwhile, we continued to try different therapists, but the full severity of his condition wasn't clear at that time.

Our family belonged to a wonderful neighborhood babysitting co-op where families would get points for taking care of other families' children. As time went on, it was more and more difficult for us to find co-op members (even friends) to care for Craig when Ken and I needed some time away. Craig questioned adult authority and that turned into a battle of wills. Ken and I didn't get to spend much time at all together without our children.

We did have fun as a family, mainly on vacations. At the time, Ken was working at a job where he had to be away a lot, but the upside was we got many frequent flier and hotel miles. We went on wonderful trips – we hiked in Colorado, and in Maine with llamas, took a Sierra club trip near Lake Tahoe, etc. Disney World was covered several times. We traveled extensively in California as well. On vacations we kept busy almost all the time, and Craig enjoyed that. He and Lindsay shared the fun, on roller-coasters and alpine slides. Craig especially loved the llamas and talked about "his" llama named Twopuk incessantly. He also wrote about 'summer memories' for a school assignment:

I hiked with 2 llamas in Maine! The llamas were named Twopuk and Omadiez. Twopuk was my favorite llama, and I really miss him. You kind of walk with llamas like a dog. A command is jiggle the leash down and they know they're going downhill. But if you walk too close to them or touch their head, they spit at you!

If their ears are straight up, they are hearing as best as they can or they are happy. If their ears are down, they want to be left alone. If you go near them when their ears are down, they spit!

On the first day, we hiked with llamas to a place where we camped out. The second day, we hiked to the top of the mountain, and I almost whammed myself in the eye with a walking stick! At the top, we could see Mount

Washington. Then we went back down and slept at the same place. And on the 3rd day, we left. When the llamas know where they are, and they're almost back where they belong (at the hotel) they go um, um, um.

What the llamas do is carry your stuff. You stop in a beautiful place to have snacks and eat. After you eat, you swim in a river. The instructors were really nice. But one of the instructors didn't go good in school (he had trouble spelling horse.)

Lots of the meals on the trip, I had ice cream. It was good! One of the places, I went down alpine slides, I played bumper cars with my dad, and lots of other fun games.

It was a great trip!

When Craig was in third grade, we vacationed at a ranch near Rocky Mountain National Park in Colorado. Craig caught a fish there - and here's the story written by Craig, age eight, about what happened next:

It all started when I went to a ranch in Colorado and I went fishing. I caught a fish and gave it to my dad. He brought it next to me. Someone who worked at the ranch took a picture of me holding a fish. I was so excited. Then later at dinner time they brought the fish to me. I started crying because I felt sorry for the fish for being killed. I insisted they take it away. I had pizza instead of the fish.

Craig Climbed a Tree

The second thing that happened a [while later] is I went to Florida and saw my grandpa for the last time. Then my dad recorded grandpa and grandma hugging and talking about how nice we were. We took a plane back to Maryland.

Then we heard that grandpa died. Our family was really upset. Then I started feeling bad about killing animals and people. I started thinking about dying a lot. Then I asked if they kill animals for food. My mother said "yes." I was really upset.

I decided that I didn't want to eat any meat, or fish. I have been a vegetarian for almost a year. I feel really good, but bad when I see people eating meat. I stopped because I knew it was killing animals, even though I liked hamburgers so much.

I think that I'm going to be a vegetarian for my whole life and get my kids to be vegetarians. Now I feel like I want to be married to a vegetarian who does not take drugs or smoke. It is very hard to be a vegetarian because I like meat a lot. When I look at meat now, I think it's disgusting.

I'd like to convince my friends to be vegetarians, and be like me!

Craig won a $50 savings bond from the Baltimore-based Vegetarian Resource Group for this essay. From the day of his decision at eight, he was a vegetarian for the rest of his life. For many years, his favorite food was toasted ravioli. It's interesting that he talks about convincing his friends to be vegetarians – his short-lived neighborhood friendships.

Generally, Craig got bored easily but when he became old enough to play Monopoly, he played it incessantly and always won. He loved the money and buying properties. Interestingly, when we didn't have time or desire to play Monopoly with him, he played it himself against an imaginary "he." Afterwards, Craig would tell us how many games he won against himself. He also liked to write, and he and Lindsay put together little stories that they sold to us for between a penny and a dime, depending on the characters. When he got old enough, Scrabble and Boggle were games he enjoyed and excelled at.

One December, when Ken was still a Divisional Vice-President for a Fortune 500 company, we surprised Lindsay and Craig by showing them some pictures of a cruise ship, and letting them know they would be going on a cruise in a week. Pretty exciting stuff! Craig had just turned twelve and Lindsay was fourteen. The cruise was fun for the family. However, one disturbing event happened when we were on-board the ship. Craig went to sleep in his underwear in our ship's room and Lindsay, Ken and I went to see a show. When we returned, Craig was awake and told us that he had been sleep-walking and a staff member had found him dressed in underwear on one of the decks. By the time she found him, he was awake but he had locked himself out of the room. She got a key and brought him back shortly before we returned. He was able to tell us the story, but still... Scary! We never left him alone again on the boat in the evening.

Chapter Two: Unexpected

Craig entered middle school with this letter to his new science teacher and 6th grade team leader:

6/6/95

Hello, I am Craig Wishnick and I'm 11 years old. I'm scared about Middle School because

A: More work

B: Older kids

C: Locker combination

I'm not sure if I'm looking forward to leaving a school I've been in for six years. Although I'm sure you will make me feel better.

I've lived in Maryland since I was three. My sister Lindsay was in your class and now is in 8th grade. She told me you tell lots of jokes. I have a dog who is very friendly named Rocky and a mom and dad named Fran and Ken. I just put five goldfish I had for 1 year in the pond. I miss them a lot. My grandpa died when I was eight. I'm a

vegetarian. I've stopped eating meat for many years!
Nobody else in my family is a vegetarian. My neighbor
Adam is in your class and says you're very nice. I'm looking
forward to meeting you.

The dreaded lockers! Here's the kid who could beat
everyone at Monopoly and Scrabble, but he was
overcome by anxiety about a locker combination that
consisted of numbers. Turns of the lock needed to be
practiced over and over again until Craig felt that he had
mastered them. Most middle-school newcomers were a
bit fearful. but for Craig, lockers, school assignments,
school electives, new relationships—the whole transition
to middle school—was truly anxiety-provoking. Craig's
carefully worded note to his new team leader didn't reflect
the full-fledged anxiety that he shared with us about
everything, from how to open his locker to going from
class to class to meeting new people.

His therapist convinced us that Craig needed an anti-
anxiety medication. We, the parents who dispensed
Ibuprofen so carefully and infrequently, agreed to try an
unknown (to us) medication on our young son. As it
turned out, there wasn't enough time to see if anti-anxiety
medication worked before the next and quite serious
problem unfolded.

Fran and Craig Wishnick

It was time for a regular physical exam for Craig, so he and I were sitting in a small room at his pediatrician's office. The doctor was examining Craig's feet and legs, when suddenly he stopped. "When did these start?" Craig had purple bruises on his legs. Some were tiny, the size and color of light freckles. Others were larger and dramatically visible. In fact, they were all over his body. We had seen the bigger ones before, and had asked him if he had hurt himself riding his bike, playing tennis or basketball, or...? He said he thought he had. However, his pediatrician was alarmed, and insisted that Craig go immediately to the lab for a blood test. I admit that I was not yet in panic mode. If anything, I thought it was some minor problem, perhaps requiring some medication.

The next morning, Craig's pediatrician called me at home. In measured words, he told me to stop everything and get Craig to Johns Hopkins Hospital in Baltimore. I had never been there before and remember driving in run-down neighborhoods, trying to carry on a casual conversation with Craig while my head was exploding. He asked me what I was doing to help people who were in such conditions, such poverty. In Craig's black-and-white thinking, he couldn't understand how people knew a problem existed but put it aside as something bigger than them, too big to solve. With my thoughts flying, I offered that maybe we could do something together, to help.

At the Pediatric Hematology unit, we learned that Craig's blood platelet count had gone down to an alarming 3,000. A normal platelet count is between 150,000 and 450,000. The bruises were purpura, the tiny bruises were petechiae, and Craig was diagnosed with Idiopathic Thrombocytopenia Purpura (ITP) – a serious disorder of the immune system of unknown cause that can result in uncontrollable bleeding. I was terrified. The doctors started him on intravenous immunoglobulin. I remember being in the room with Craig when he had the first intravenous treatment. Other children undergoing treatment were quietly watching videos; Craig had great difficulty tolerating the process and we felt like it went on forever. When the procedure didn't have the desired effect, he was placed on a high dose of steroids and was permitted to return to school, with a doctor's note prescribing restricted physical activity and extensive monitoring. They also took Craig off anti-anxiety medication, since his doctors couldn't rule out that it caused the ITP.

Over the next few months, his platelet counts gradually returned to normal and he was permitted to engage in physical activity. However, the reduced but still high levels of steroid resulted in depression—a not uncommon side effect, especially for someone already prone to depression. The hematologist was cautious about lowering the steroids, and definitely not ready to take Craig off of them.

With the lowering of the steroids came another blow—a more common immune system problem called Ulcerative Colitis. Although there was some history of colitis in our family, Craig developed severe rectal bleeding. Although the doctors initially tried other medication, he had to go back on high doses of steroids.

This was so stressful for Craig, Lindsay, and Ken and me. Even now, it's difficult for me to think back on just how traumatic it was. We didn't know where to turn. Ken and I struggled to function day-to-day. We tried as hard as we could not to, but Lindsay got less attention than Craig. She was "the older sister who needed to understand." We knew it at the time, but as we look back now, it's even clearer that Craig's problems and family stress were very difficult for her.

Craig's medical problems resulted in our frequently questioning him about how he felt, whether he had bleeding, and whether he had examined himself for petechiae. Questioning him felt uncomfortable. It was invasive, especially when puberty and independence from parents was just beginning. When Craig told us about the bleeding, it was difficult for him to describe how much. What constitutes a lot or a little? He wanted the criteria defined down to minute detail.

Academically, Craig didn't have the typical middle school problem of time management in completing assignments. However, he had a major problem in understanding non-literal texts like mythology. He and I spent countless hours trying to understand it together. He became incensed when I couldn't explain it to his satisfaction, yet he was so focused on completing assignments that he stuck with it, and so did I.

Craig struggled with the idea of similarities in essays that he needed to write, especially for his English class. For example, Craig never understood the saying, "You're comparing apples and oranges." To him, apples and oranges were fruit that grew on trees, had pits, etc. He insisted that there should be a formula to decide when objects were similar. Since his teachers didn't think this way, I had to convince him, again and again, to count objects as similar if there were some traits that they had in common. Over the years, we "discussed" this many times.

He often had difficulty completing assignments at home independently, especially if there were complex, non-sequential directions. He required many hours of parental support and supervision in understanding content. Even so, he maintained excellent grades, because he was totally committed to doing so. Private tutoring was not a solution, since his confusion was not subject-specific but rather direction- and language-specific.

He asked us a lot of questions, all day long. I've already mentioned that Craig was always interested in money; I saved one piece that he wrote around age twelve:

I am really sorry about bothering my dearest parents about money (I am not just saying this.) I would never like my nice parents to ever be upset with me about money ever again. Therefore, I am setting some rules which I will follow:

☐ *I get two warnings per day from both of you two combined to stop talking about money. If I don't stop after the 2 warnings, $3 of my allowance will explode each time this happens.*

I will try to remember to write my questions about money down on a piece of paper. Each Friday night around 6:30 I will ask you and dad for money or questions about money. If I forget to write the questions down or keep bugging you, you know the consequence.

I will really try hard not to hurt my loving parents feelings again. I made 2 copies of this paper so you and I can keep one. I have learned my lesson and I would tremendously appreciate if you take off the punishment about not being able to go to Hermans (a sporting goods store)

Craig signed the note and then wrote:

PLEASE FORGIVE ME. I HAD A LOT OF GUTS TO WRITE THIS LETTER!

As much as school was a challenge for Craig, at least it provided him with routine. When summer rolled around, he faced the transition from structured school environment to unstructured time. He didn't do well without structure.

We decided to try a camp for several weeks. The medication for his colitis appeared to keep it under control, and despite both social and medical problems as the weeks progressed, the camp experience was undoubtedly one of the high points of his life. Some quotes from letters that we saved:

I have been asked by others to play tennis, ping-pong etc with them.

Thank you so much for these faxes. I really do appreciate it. However, I need more envelopes, stamps and paper in order to continue to respond.

Fran and Craig Wishnick

We will have 2 out of camp trips; one this Sunday to the Appalachian Mountains and one the last week to Adventure World.

The food is really getting revolting. And to top it off, they are claiming you never called about me being a vegetarian. They are doing this nonsense with many other people, including counselors, so it will probably be worked out within the next week.

The activities are limited right now, but they are still very fun. So far, I have done some tennis and photography. I actually like photography more because it is very interesting to see the image suddenly appear on paper after dipping it in liquids.

The counselors are interesting to say the least. Their accents make them hard to understand. They seem friendly and fun to be with but are extremely weird.

It seems so weird to be sleeping away for so long. I can't tell whether I miss you or anything. It just feels very different. I am continuing to play with others but most already knew each other from previous years.

However, despite these positive experiences, Craig's colitis flared, and from the middle of his camp program to the end, Craig spent time in the nurse's office. Plus, his confusion with relating to his peers increased as the camp season went on. We got a number of calls from him and from the camp, and by the end he was a wreck.

The year that Craig went to summer camp was a transitional one for our family for another reason. Ken had been a Divisional Vice President for a Fortune 500 company for twelve years. After receiving a stellar review and bonus the prior year, they downsized, and he was dismissed, along with many employees of all ranks. Their shareholders weren't happy with the company's stock performance. We tried to minimize the impact on Lindsay and Craig, but they knew and I'm sure they felt our stress. We told them money was tight, and that our whole family needed to stick together.

We ended up buying a small business, which we kept for a little over a year and sold at a small profit. Meanwhile, due to Craig's excellent grades, the school system decided to dismiss him from special education services.

Chapter Three: Wilby

Craig had a life-long love of animals. We always had at least one dog, and at times fish, guinea pigs, and ferrets. The ferrets were a big compromise for me, since I really didn't like them or their smell, but Lindsay and Craig promised to take care of them—a promise we had to remind them about frequently.

During Lindsay's late middle school and high school years, she had a series of pet-sitting jobs. One week, when she was away, Craig took over the care of the animals. Lindsay had taught him to write notes each day to the owners. One owner, Mrs. C., had a dog named Wilby. She thought the notes on napkins were so cute that she saved them:

—*Wilby was really fun to play with today. After the walk, I chased after Wilby in the kitchen. He ran away, then came back and lied down across the floor with this really cute look on his face. Then I chased him, and the pattern continued all over again. I really want a dog like Wilby!*

—I dried Wilby's feet as good as I could, but he wouldn't let me touch each foot for more than ½ a second. I put the towel back on top of the dryer, since I didn't know where else to put it. I would have put it in the washer, but I didn't know where the detergent was kept.

Can I move into this house, and maybe you can keep Wilby here???Just kidding, although I wish that could happen.

—It was so humid today that I could only get Wilby about ½ way to the pond. He made me feel so guilty when I pulled on the leash; he sat down and stared at me. It's only slightly more humid today, so it's confusing why he goes from one extreme to the other. Nevertheless, Wilby is one happy dog!

Chapter Four: Truths and Fears

Craig's freshman high school year continued to follow the same pattern—excellent grades obtained through his incredible effort, plus countless hours of parental support. His classes included: Honors English, Modern World History Honors, Integrated Algebra/Geometry, Life Fitness/Health, Drama 1, and Spanish 2 Honors (he loved Spanish!). He received all A's.

Unfortunately, I didn't keep much of his writing from that year. For some reason, an assignment from his Health class on "writing persuasively in a few sentences" was saved. The assignment was to think of a school policy that should be changed. Craig wrote:

I think that having Health class to teach kids to lay off drugs is dumb. It just convinces teenagers to do it more if they are told not to do it. Teenagers who take drugs don't care about school. The people who don't take drugs before the class probably won't end up taking drugs. The time could be used for academic classes instead.

Socially, Craig continued to flounder. His new manly voice had a bit of a higher pitch than normal and he was teased for that, as well as for things he said and did. He just couldn't connect with his peers. In an undated piece, Craig explained his isolation in terms that many of us can understand:

The teacher tells people to pair off in twos to work together on an assignment. Some quickly group with another based on friendships and previous interactions. Others choose the person right next to them without thinking. Yet others are searching until the pool of people narrows & then they socialize at the last moment. Now all are in pairs. All except one. The teacher asks around to see if any of the groups of 2 will accept a 3rd person. Most are too engaged in interacting to hear the teacher's message. Some look concerned but then try to ignore that they heard anything or do not feel like reaching out to this individual. Finally, one group says they'd be willing to allow this individual in. During the group work, however, the kindness fades and little attention is paid to that individual's ideas. Eventually, the assignment is completed and some new relationships are formed and some may end but that individual remains the same as before.

Reading that piece still makes me want to hold him tightly. It makes me cry.

Meanwhile, Ken and I decided to make a life-change and move to western Maryland. Ken took a new job, while Lindsay finished her senior high school year and Craig completed his freshman year. Lindsay had her college acceptance and was ready to go. Although we knew that transitions were difficult, we fervently hoped that the change in environment from suburbs to rural would be less stressful for Craig and that he could have a fresh start with his peers. In June 1999, we moved to western Maryland.

Craig wrote a note to a California relative in April of 1999:

> *Sorry I haven't written to you in so long. I've just been busy with school work and packing up to move to (a place in Maryland). I'm going to be moving there as soon as this school year ends. It's going to be a lot different... They only have two high schools – a northern and a southern. I'm going to the northern high school... The house that we bought ... has six acres of basically flat land and a lot of trees. I'm thinking of many different things I could put there like a basketball court, volleyball net or a hammock. I'll also be getting a job ... as soon as I move there... There are many exciting things about moving there*

but it's just going to be very interesting because I haven't moved since I was two or three years old...

I remember driving there, and casually talking with Craig about his new high school, which he had already toured. We spoke about how the environment was going to be less liberal than where had been raised. I remember saying that people were likely to ask him which church he belonged to (we are from a Jewish background). In Craig's fashion, he quickly said, "I'll tell them I'm home-churched." He had developed skills and a sense of humor about putting words and ideas together creatively.

Shortly after we moved, we helped Craig get a restaurant job. However, he couldn't work fast enough or follow multi-step directions and his colitis was flaring again. He had to stop. As the summer progressed, his colitis got worse. His primary care doctor tried a variety of medications, but Craig was experiencing lots of pain and stomach contractions.

One evening it was especially bad and nothing we tried brought him relief. Around midnight, we decided I would take Craig back to Baltimore to the Johns Hopkins Emergency Room—a 4-hour drive from our new home. Lindsay came along, to do whatever she could to help. After a full examination, the pediatric gastroenterologist took me aside and said that while his colitis condition was undoubtedly flaring and was significant, she believed that there was also a psychiatric component to his suffering. Craig stayed at Hopkins for several days while they attempted to stabilize the colitis. Upon discharge with heavy duty colitis medication, doctors also strongly recommended that he be put on an antidepressant again. The last time he had been on one was in middle school, weeks before he got that immune system disorder called ITP. We were hesitant, but knew we had no choice. We had to do something.

We started the antidepressant shortly before Lindsay was to leave for college in August. Things got much worse just a few days before she left, just as Craig was to begin his sophomore year at his new high school. Although the bleeding from Craig's colitis had subsided somewhat, the pain had not. Lindsay and Craig were getting into more prolonged arguments, including one about the need for him to take care of their two ferrets while she was in college.

One evening, Craig's lifelong suicidal ideations worsened to the point that he started staring at electrical wires and, with horrible looks of desperation on his face, needed to be held back from wrapping them around his neck. We took him to a psychiatric hospital, about an hour away. Every second of that ride is embedded in my mind.

Craig Climbed a Tree

Craig was admitted to the adolescent psychiatric unit. He was 15 years old. Ken, Lindsay and I drove home in full despair.

A few days later, I took Lindsay to her out-of-state college. Although glad to be there, she had felt all the emotions of Craig's decline that summer and our eyes were locked and tearful when I dropped her off. I hoped that she would find people who understood. At that point, that was all I could do.

Meanwhile, in the hospital, Craig was put on a number of medications. He didn't look good and he was still suicidal. Frankly, we didn't have faith that the psychiatrist was properly evaluating and treating him. Plus, their in-patient program automatically provided him with mandatory drug and alcohol education because studies have shown that depressed teenagers are likely to use drug and alcohol. But Craig wasn't a typical teenager. Craig openly mocked the hospital's drug and alcohol education and predictably, the negative reactions from staff further compounded his stress.

A few days later, the psychiatrist and social worker at the hospital told us that our private insurance had denied an additional hospital stay by re-categorizing Craig's condition as chronic, not acute. We never had insurance problems before—but then again, we had never experienced psychiatric hospitalization for a family member before. There was something important that we didn't know about our policy: our insurer had subcontracted with a managed care behavioral health agency. This subcontractor was impossible to work with—they wouldn't return calls, every time we called them they told us that Craig had a new "case manager." We learned that our policy didn't pay for chronic mental health care. The insurer was not cooperative or sympathetic to the fact that our teenage son, never before hospitalized, was still highly suicidal.

We met with the doctors and all agreed that Craig could not be discharged. Weeks later, we got a retroactive denial of his stay, with a bill for tens of thousands. That bill was eventually reversed through my advocacy, but it was unbelievably frustrating and added to our family's overloaded stress level.

Subsequently, Craig was hospitalized on and off at three different hospitals, as an inpatient and in day programs, from August 28, 1999 to November 12, 1999. We had to take him out of the second hospital against medical advice when it became clear that their primary clientele was teens with behavioral problems. The staff wouldn't even provide him with vegetarian meals until I fought and cried. It was horrible. Thinking about it now makes me shake. Any time we drove anywhere near there, years later, Craig trembled and asked for reassurance that he wasn't going back.

Meanwhile, Craig had missed the first few months of school and it was unclear whether he should or could return. On October 14, 1999 he wrote:

One of the hardest things in life is to prove who you are. It doesn't just have to be convincing yourself, although that is very important. Others have expectations that you need to follow, all these rules and guidelines to almost anything that happens. I feel that along with satisfying everybody else by doing this, there is additional pressure to exceed what others expect. Some of the pressure has to deal with the fact that I want to be different than normal people, to somehow inspire everyone to think differently. But then I wonder if I'm trying to control everyone and that maybe I should just withdraw myself from society, so I won't be causing any harm.

One of the biggest stressors right now is the possibility of going to school. I really would enjoy learning, just because it's fun to challenge myself to things I know can be accomplished. It wouldn't hurt my reputation or anything, probably even boost my self-esteem. The big problem is the social aspect, introducing myself and going through the terrible process of having my peers get to know me. I'm so self-conscious of what they'd want me to be that I try and be too perfect. It's not within my control right now to just get myself to calm down; I'm really frightened of what others think of me, to the point where I've give up almost anything for others just to further understand and accept me. And I really can't get to just introducing myself because just previous to a situation like that, I have a panic attack, so my body shakes like crazy and I sometimes become suicidal.

Basically, right now I'm living because society won't tolerate someone committing suicide. If I had my way though, I would have been dead a long time ago. Life is tiring, stressful, and continually has unpleasant situations that come up which I have trouble getting out of my head. The thoughts are repetitious, especially at night since it's dark, and darkness reminds me of being lonely and isolated from the outside world. If there was any way that I could just satisfy others – it seems like they always want more than I can do. Does that mean I'm selfish, that I don't try hard enough, or just don't deserve to live? Probably all of the above.

I know most of my thoughts are kind of messed up, that my body looks for stressful situations and keys into them...

Craig Climbed a Tree

In another piece that Craig called "Questions and Answers":

1. What do others expect of me that is so stressful? – Sometimes to believe in the same religion as them, to be social, and to at least fake being cheerful (don't walk around being so depressed all of the time.)

2. What are the positive things in life? – Making others happy, doing recreational activities, having caring and supportive friends, family and relatives, listening to music, to see all of the interesting places in the world, buying bargain stuff off the internet, to just be seen as a hard worker, and to possibly influence others with my opinions.

3. What are the negative things in life? – All the struggles and tough times that people have to go through. It also seems like there's no point to living. It doesn't seem like life is worth all the hard work and challenges.

4. You have your whole life to live – why are you giving up so soon? Things will get better even though it doesn't seem like that now. – Yeah right! 15 years is a long time even though a natural life span is about 75 years. I've had enough of all this torture, of how incredibly boring and pointless life is.

5. Don't you want to get married and raise children? – Why would I? Then I'd be continuing the boring traditions of our society, even though there are small periods of time where there is joy.

6. What about your family and all the people that care about you so much? – That helps me quite a bit while I'm living. But I still know that life has too many struggles, and it's not worth it to continue. I can't just live for others – it has to be for myself too. And I have very little self-esteem and encouragement to go on...

In yet another piece, Craig wrote:

I think that I will try again to go to school, study, etc. BUT this can only be done if I know that I have a fall-back, just in case things don't work out. That fall-back, at least right now, is not following the vigorous challenges that life has. Without some type of fall-back, I cannot continue knowing there isn't a second choice, at the moment, if life proves to be too stressful for me. I cannot be faulted or yelled at, no matter which path I choose. I cannot be considered responsible for how others are

Craig Climbed a Tree

affected by my situation...I have to be allowed to weigh the options and consider what is best for my situation.

Our minds were reeling and our hearts were broken. We were frightened, isolated, and at our wits' end. We didn't know where to turn or what to do. Craig was 15 years old.

Chapter Five: Next

Craig did return to school, under circumstances that would challenge almost anyone: starting at a brand new school, having missed several months of classes, assignments and connections. Given his recent psychiatric history and how Craig's issues and history were unknown to them, the teachers, guidance counselors and administrators were not prepared to have him there. And, although I had been in touch with the school while Craig was hospitalized and submitted documentation of the cause of his absences, initially the school system said Craig could not get credit for the school year because he had exceeded the number of allowable absences. The school attempted to give Craig very limited time to make up work for all the days he was absent and wanted him to take lower level courses than he wanted. At Craig's request (but always wondering if we were doing the right thing), we got a time extension plus the reinstatement of classes for which Craig had originally signed up.

Craig got to work. With massive parental support and Craig's internal desire, his intellectual strengths and perseverance, he made up all the assignments within several weeks and ultimately received excellent grades for the semester.

That's the good news. The horrible piece was that on most days Craig would go to school, come home and do his assignments—then express suicidal thoughts in the evenings. It kept him and us awake until deep into the dark night. It was horrendous beyond description. We reported all this to his psychiatrist, who was also in communication with the school. Often, I felt certain that Craig wouldn't be able to go back to school, or shouldn't go, but he did. Learning was the only life-task where Craig felt successful. For several months, Craig had a monitor accompany him from class to class due to concerns about his emotional condition, and he was put in a special education homeroom class.

Craig went to the health room when he couldn't handle what was going on his head, where he benefitted from expressing himself in writing. Here's an example that I found, a note Craig sent to his science teacher:

Thank you very much for spending time during your 6ᵗʰ period planning to discuss possible strategies that I could use to effectively present my role as the County Sanitation Commissioner in front of the class. You gave me very helpful ideas to consider such as answering questions until I am no longer able to, and then have Joe answer the rest.

Although strategies such as that could help me in the presentation, I am still tormented with stress and anxiety over the situation. The idea of just standing in front of the class for a couple of seconds is a really scary thought to me, and it has continually proved troublesome with my ability to focus during class time and outside of school. I think it might be a better idea not to do the presentation because negative ideas and thoughts and continually accumulating about how I could mess up in the presentation.

Thus, unless I am able to control these negative feelings by class, I believe it would be best for me to spend 5ᵗʰ period in the health room. ... Please understand that, in this situation, I am not skipping class for some reason other than my emotional condition. Again, if I feel by 5ᵗʰ period that I can do the presentation in front of the class, I definitely will come in and try my best. Thanks for your understanding.

He added a footnote:

Craig Climbed a Tree

I am attaching to this paper the opening statement, defense on cross examinations, cross examinations of other groups, and the concluding statement. Please give the papers to Joe so he can present on behalf of the County Sanitation Commission in front of the class.

I was glad that he was able to articulate the problems, but dismayed at how his anxiety and stress affected every aspect of his life.

Just before Craig turned 17, we paid for an evaluation of his neuropsychological functioning and potential learning disability. We needed to understand what was happening and what to expect. Tests showed a significant weakness in abstract-visual reasoning, but strong auditory short-term memory and listening skills. Academic performance achievement was at or above the level expected given his age and grade level. His weakest performance showed difficulties with oral expression, and comprehension of abstract concepts. The testing "...suggests that he has been able to maintain high academic achievement only through an excessive level of effort and external support." It also showed difficulty with "...his ability to inhibit impulsive responses to auditory stimuli."

At the time of the testing, the examiner reported that Craig was "...experiencing low mood, a bleak view of his future, very low self-esteem, some sleep problems and intermittent suicidal ideation (without a plan.)" Without a plan is terminology used to evaluate the level of suicide risk at a given point in time. Having a specific suicide plan such as overdosing on drugs points to a higher risk than thoughts without a plan.

A diagnosis of Asperger's Syndrome was made based on: " 1) awkwardness with peer interactions and excessive difficulty in making and maintaining peer friendships; 2) difficulty and anxiety around maintaining conversation (3) expressive and receptive communication deficits...4) lack of imaginative play or typical toy use when younger; 5) obsessional focus on single topics 6) difficulty with transitions or changes...7) mildly odd use of words or phrases including phrases that are not quite appropriate or relevant to the context at hand; 8) hypersensitivity for sound, touch, taste and smell to the point that he can become distracted or distressed by sensory perceptions that others may not even notice."

This was the first time that a medical professional had diagnosed Craig with Asperger's.

The examiner recommended specialized placement in a therapeutic educational setting, with Asperger's professionals. She specified that the setting should "...augment Craig's curriculum with the specific special education and language aids required for him to succeed without the excessive effort and dependency upon his parents...required now."

During a special education meeting about Craig at the school, we teleconferenced in that examiner, a high-level medical professional. The results weren't good. The school system wouldn't recommend or fund a therapeutic placement. Craig couldn't tolerate the idea that we would pay for private schooling, nor did he accept that such a therapeutic educational setting could be a fit for him. He wrote:

I have seen many psychiatrists and they will not and claim they "cannot" help me if I do not change my ways of viewing life. For the most part, I am unwilling to change. Of course, I am interested in the logic that people use to convince me of reasons to change, but I can easily counter those arguments and show that they do not make sense. More often than not, these viewpoints have a dark side to them that is not immediately noticeable due to the "think positively" outlook of psychiatrists.

Do not be hypnotized by a well-worded mission statement or beautiful scenery at a facility. In addition, when you meet a friendly staff person, that individual is frequently not reflective of the overall staff at the facility. Instead, when making a decision, look at the core of that place and see what it really offers. Ask yourself, "How does this place deviate from the others that I have read about or visited. Do I really know enough about the place, or am I just hearing the aspects that they want me to hear?"

Any place that says my beliefs are a "problem" is completely out of touch. Why won't these people work with me and accept my beliefs, rather than saying, "We are going to assimilate you into a civilized, normal, or more healthy or productive lifestyle?"

We felt profoundly stuck. We would have tried just about anything to help our son.

Socially, Craig vacillated between trying to engage with his peers, while feeling unsuccessful and saying that he had no interest in having friends. He continued to love animals, and convinced us to foster dogs that were being put up for adoption. It didn't take much convincing. We love dogs and we were willing to do anything reasonable that would calm Craig. Mainly, we did short-term fostering of purebreds from animal shelters in hopes of finding homes. Eventually, we fostered and adopted a mixed breed whose name, Scruffy, fit her well. Craig often called her "Baby Girl," or sometimes "Communist." Craig adored Scruffy and treated her with upmost gentleness. She did the same for him. Whenever his colitis flared, he would call her over and she would lie down precisely on the spot that was hurting him. Their connection over many years was truly profound. This wonderful animal had a gentle soul.

Craig still had one ferret. One day, rather impulsively, he took the ferret—off leash—for a walk in the woods behind our home. The ferret ran away and Craig came back to the house, face ashen and body shaking. I couldn't reassure him that we'd ever see the ferret again. I was pretty angry that he had done this and that he wanted me to go into the woods and find it. Miraculously, a few hours later, we heard a scratch at the back door. Our ferret had returned!

Yet, Craig's depression and anxiety continued to rage. He wrote:

I dreamt that there was an extremely deep and lengthy water. Waves about 10 feet high were moving along rapidly. It was estimated that there were hundreds and hundreds of sharks at the location I was near. I was standing in this area with lots of trees, as a group of teenagers were shivering cold, even me, very nervous about what would happen next. Our camp instructor was very mean but all of us, campers, never expected that we'd be in an area as scary as this.

To make it even worse, we woke up one morning and the instructor said something that terrified us all. "Get moving, you're going across the water," he yelled. If you stay here, I'll torture you for the rest of your life. But if you get to the other side of the ocean, your families will be there to rescue you all afterwards. Oh, and just to let you know, 1 out of every 40 people on average get across (because of the sharks, and also how long the ocean is.)" Everybody was terrified, especially since there were exactly 40 of us, so one person would only get across.

There is a lot of symbolism here in the dream that I had. The sharks and the instructor represent the torture and all the terrifying things people have to go through in order to be successful. Crossing the ocean represents becoming an individual, with nobody to support you but yourself. I really don't want to think about this anymore because it really gets me scared and extremely worried.

That essay, Craig's thoughts, shook us up more than ever—but again, we didn't know what to do. Craig attended school, was compliant on medication, and saw his psychiatrist and therapist. His therapist told him he needed to try to think more positively. Craig wrote:

I am finding myself alive day after day,
Having to endure struggle after struggle.

Craig Climbed a Tree

Everyone else says it depends on how you view the situation,
You can either view it positively or negatively,
That it depends on how you want to feel.
I want to feel like I am away from life itself,
Where I am found of having a disability,
Yet the help I receive is of little benefit,
For I am treated like one who is clueless.
One who does not know the difference between the words "ancient" and "modern"
Or perhaps with simply a few internal problems,
For which it is believed that I just need to change my ways.
But of course I am reminded that there is no "magic cure".
If there was magic, I obviously would not be here now.

People say a God exists, that justice exists,
Yet the death penalty is what I aim for,
And instead it is used for punishment towards criminals,
People who did "horrible acts"
They get honored but do not appreciate such honor.
But of course, as long as people don't want what they're getting it's okay,

As long as a lesson is taught,
As long as the welfare of the people is okay.
Any person that does not agree obviously is at a poor
mental state.
The people are not okay
Or at least not myself.
I am accused of having depression,
And I do not dispute that,
For life is definitely full of enough stress to fill
anyone with depression.
But for doctors to tell me I need to change,
To repeat obvious things like change happens over
time,
Or question if I want to stay the way I am,
If I want to wake up happy or upset.
My character is being demolished,
My self-perception along with my motivation.
What happens next?
Of course, the perfect solution-
I am loaded with additional stress each day,
Somehow, whether at school or at home,
And I am then asked why I do this to myself?
The better question is why does society do this to me?
This is not to mention the impact on others.
Others who have to deal with me every day.

With the pressure that I put them through,
Having to work with a kid that obviously has mental
problems.
How could anyone ask this of a human being?
Better yet, why does society have to deal with me?
Why am I forced to go through a painful life,?
As I only pass on pain to myself and others.
It does not matter the point of view I am born with,
Or the point of view I have throughout my life,
Any living being,
Knowing what I go through,
Know what others go through because of me,
Should realize that I should be assisted in ending life
itself,
And that is not through a life in hospitals.

Hope, despair, more despair, feelings of isolation, lack of sleep—we lived with Craig, cared about him, understood his stresses, loved him —but were barely able to deal with all this daily depression and anxiety. We wanted desperately to help and constantly searched for resources. We saw no other choice, as we plodded along, lacking in sleep and confidence and emotionally spent.

Meanwhile, Craig had grown weary of the environment at his high school, and asked to spend his senior high school year at a community college. His social studies teacher prepared the following recommendation:

I am recommending that Craig Wishnick be considered for the Early College Admission Program. I have worked with Craig this year as his A.P. United States History teacher. At the present time, Craig has an A in the course. He has an outstanding analytical mind. Craig works very hard to maintain good grades in all his classes. He turns in all his work on time and is very prepared for each class. History is one of his main interests and Craig has related to me that he wants to pursue this at the college level. Craig is very dependable and reliable. If he says he will do something, you can count on it being done and done well. He has a fine work ethic and takes his studies seriously. He has an inquisitive mind and seeks out information that helps his daily lesson preparation. These are qualities that potential college students need and Craig has these. Craig Wishnick should be considered for the Early College Admission Program.

Chapter Six: Baths

On September 11, 2001, I watched the news coverage of the twin tower tragedy with Craig. His worldview was already pretty dismal and the events that unfolded merged with and enhanced his pessimistic life perspective.

Some people with mental health challenges self-mutilate, by "cutting." Some abuse drugs or alcohol, others are violent, or go off medications. Craig didn't engage in any of those behaviors. However, late at night he would sometimes take a rope or whatever he could find and squeeze it around his neck, occasionally leaving telling red marks. He would even come into our room in the middle of the night to show us. We were unable to go back to sleep or think clearly for days on end.

Crying for help, manipulation, or unable to control his impulses, or all of the above? We had already gone the hospitalization route in several different hospitals, the therapist and psychiatrist route, with medication, etc. Craig was saying he would finish high school and then kill himself because he could not envision his personal future. Our distress level was highly elevated, not far below his. He was clearly telling us that he had a not-too-distant plan to end his life.

Even in hindsight, thinking about that time all over again, I don't have a "should have" perspective for what we might have done differently during that period. We read and researched, spoke to anyone who would listen, to try to find answers—and hoped, prayed for insight and strength.

I've been asked if we were able to network with parents of other similar children. The answer is no, though we certainly tried. Repeatedly, parents of other troubled youth would tell us that we should be glad that our child didn't abuse alcohol or drugs, wasn't in the prison system, hadn't dropped out of school. "Yes," we screamed in our heads, Craig was different—but deeply troubled nonetheless, and we needed help. For him, and yes, for us.

To calm himself, Craig often listened to music, favoring folk protest songs of the 60s, Latin American music, even opera. He also took long baths and ordered bath oils and lotions to make them more soothing. It's comforting to think back to the times he would be researching on-line, trying to get "deals" on stuff that seemed like extravagances. Nonetheless, since he didn't allow us to give him birthday or occasion gifts, we thought of these products as gifts, and were grateful to hear of anything that minimized his anxieties.

At complete odds with his stated plan to end his life, he applied to other schools, while enrolled in the community college (under early college admission) during his senior high school year. Unfortunately, we retain very few writings by Craig from that year. One e-mail, to us, relates his experience in a Sociology class that he took:

Today, we played a review game in Sociology class where we were put into groups, and each person would get a question and write down the first 3 letters of the answer and put the paper up in the air more quickly than the person in each of the other groups. Then the paper would be passed around. The individual with the most correct answers would get 5 bonus points.

I think you might find this interesting. It normally takes more about ¼ of a second to think of the answer and many seconds to write down the answer and raise the paper. I decided that 5 extra credit points would be worth a lot of anxiety, so I made myself go into a panic mode and not enjoy the game. By doing so, I was able to increase my speed a whole lot in writing down the answer, so it only took me about a second in total. I won the game by far and earned 5 extra credit points. Had I not gotten myself into this panic mode, I would not have received the extra credit. However, I am having difficulty calming myself down now.

We wondered about his ability to control his anxiety. Actually, that was always a major question for us—to what extent, if any, was Craig inducing his own anxiety/depression cycle? What, if anything, could be done about it? In the example above, he described consciously getting himself into a souped-up anxiety state. That "prize" of extra credit that he knew was attainable was too much for him to knowingly turn down. He was always focused on those grades.

During the year at the community college, I continued to advocate, a few times, in classes where he couldn't do the assignment. He had reached the age when he needed to be able to handle this himself but we also recognized his fragile state. I encouraged him to obtain subject-specific tutoring at the college, but as I described earlier, the material that he didn't understand was usually language- or directions-specific. Eventually, I intervened with two of the professors, in an attempt to explain why he required alternative assignments. Ken and I both continued to help Craig understand some basics, like how a right angle could be drawn to the left and still be counted as a right angle. That was but one example of his literal black-and-white thinking.

When Craig turned eighteen, we decided to apply for Supplemental Security Income (SSI) for him. It was heartbreakingly clear to us that he was an ill young man who needed services. Our research showed us he would get a cash payment, Medicaid and possibly some vocational rehabilitation services. He could also get food stamps, but that wasn't a concern for us at the time. We had never imagined that we would have a child on disability, but there we were. The SSI disability application was arduous for Craig, and for us, because Craig had to relate details of how he felt during the day. He dictated the answers to us over several days. When asked if he needed help preparing meals, he said:

Trouble with multi-step directions, fear of fire, need for perfection, directions often seem ambiguous.

When prompted to describe his shopping, he related:

Due to my obsessiveness with saving money and my fear of being with crowds, I prefer to shop on the internet and stay home. Because I can get lost or have panic attacks, I always stay with my parents when going to big stores or malls. I can't bring myself to ask workers where to find items.

And when asked how he gets along with others, he responded:

I don't feel any special attachment to others. It is better to prevent relationships than to be trapped by them. I can get along with others if they don't smoke, the directions are very clear, small talk is avoided and they are understanding of my need for short breaks and a flexible pace.

Soon after the Social Security Administration received all required paperwork, his application for SSI was approved. Next, we talked with everyone we could about a possible therapeutic location where he could go after finishing high school. Such a place was in my dreams for him and yet I doubted that it existed. Fortunately, an acquaintance had heard of a community in New England. She didn't know much about it, except that it was for people eighteen years and older who had mental health challenges and had a farm where clients could work with animals. Based on that information, and little else but desperate hope mixed with apprehension, we arranged for a special caretaker for Craig while Ken and I traveled to that special farm community.

Chapter Seven: Wishes, Sighs, and Llamas

As we entered the farm grounds, we saw their sign about harvesting hope. Sighing deeply, Ken and I drove up to Main House and met the Admissions Director, a gentle woman we instantly liked. As she took us around, we were struck by the kindness and low-key nature of the community. I'll always remember the moment when the Admissions Director said, "They're all our sons – aren't they?" We lost it and cried—about Craig, and everything he and our family had gone through: our isolation from others who understood, wanting and needing a place where Craig could be accepted, and hoping he might begin to feel a sense of purpose. It all came out—our tears were about so many things.

We liked the farm enough to believe that it wouldn't be harmful to Craig. We hoped it would be beneficial. We left with an understanding that if we could convince Craig to try it out for two weeks, during his spring break, they were willing to give him a try. We knew if we pushed Craig at all, he wouldn't go.

Upon returning home, we watched the farm video again privately and then told Craig about the community, the animals we had seen there, and the absence of pressures. He immediately asked for the website address, went to the computer, and spent about two hours in a locked room. When he finally came out, he seemed surprised and subdued. He said he didn't see anything on the website that made him concerned and announced he would try it. We were amazed, but didn't want to show too much enthusiasm for fear it might turn him away from this plan.

Several weeks later, I brought Craig to the farm. Because of his history and suicidal ideations and actions, I was asked to stay in the general area of the farm for his two week stay, while they evaluated whether he was appropriate as a guest. During that time, I traveled around, exploring the area—but always in touch with the staff and my husband Ken. We learned that Craig was isolating at the farm, spending most of his days with the llamas and other animals and avoiding social interactions of any kind. However, he was all right, and that was good enough. At the conclusion of the two- week trial period, the farm said that he could come back that summer.

Fran and Craig Wishnick

On the drive back home with Craig, I wanted to hear about his experiences, but held myself back from asking a lot of questions. I didn't ask if he wanted to return there. It was so difficult. It was important to me that Craig's answer be "yes." He had received several college acceptances, but we knew college wasn't something he could do yet or maybe ever. We had slowly altered any expectations we had about his future. Our hopes were for Craig to find peace and maybe some joy.

He needed a therapeutic environment that would accept him as he was and help him to understand his strengths, to feel a sense of purpose. It's important to add that we needed it to work out financially for us. We were and are middle-class people and most places we had researched had costs that were completely impossible for us. Fortunately, the farm offered financial aid that made it possible for us to send him there.

Before the summer began, I wrote a note to the farm staff. It reads, in part:

We are very pleased that Craig will be with all of you at the farm for the next several months and know this really has the potential for being a life-changing experience for him (and us.)

Craig Climbed a Tree

As you engage Craig in your many activities, we thought it might be helpful to the team to have our wish list for his program.

☐ *Flexibility – Craig forms an expectation of how everything in life should happen, down to the minutest of details. When things don't occur as anticipated, anxiety will follow and usually at levels that are tremendously out of proportion to the deviation i.e. if he has convinced himself that a particular piece of mail will arrive on a particular day, its absence might result in seclusion and deep depression for a period of time. We find that he experiences very little ability to deal with unpredicted or overwhelming situations and that what is overwhelming for him is often run of the mill for neuro-typical people. He sees life in general as very stressful, pointless and frustrating. We are hoping that his stay at the farm results in an increased ability to deal with daily life situations and challenges.*

☐ *Ability to Accept Social Interactions – If a person engages Craig in conversation, he may do okay in the dialogue and appear fine on the surface. However, he then retreats with great anxiety and expresses discomfort and anger over being involved in "small talk." At night, he reviews all his "mistakes" over and over in his head. We are hoping that his stay at the farm results in an increased ability to deal with people. Our fondest hope is that he learns to experience some enjoyment in being with others.*

☐ *Reassessment of Medications ...*

They also asked for a parent narrative that listed points about Craig's personality, including:

☐ *Is worried what others think of him.*

☐ *Will not answer the phone*

☐ *Is obsessed about saving money – specifically looking for coupons and bargains. Pressures us to take advantage of sales, but seems to get little satisfaction from it.*

☐ *Expects those around him to remember everything he has ever told them. Gets very annoyed if he is asked to repeat himself.*

☐ *Expects all questions asked of him to have a specific purpose that he can understand.*

☐ *Works very hard and focuses on something he understands and is committed to.*

☐ *Baths with scented oils calm him. He sometimes will bathe five times a day (We understand that this is not a possibility at the farm!!)*

☐ *Especially good at word games.*

☐ *If a rule or policy doesn't make sense to him, he will debate its merit endlessly until he either agrees with it or it is changed.*

☐ *Craig is pretty good about taking his medication. We monitor this since he will sometimes forget or even drop a pill or leave one left in the cup inadvertently.*

Shortly before Craig arrived at the farm for the summer, the Admissions Director wrote to him, reporting that one of the llamas that Craig had cared for had broken his leg and the veterinarian could not repair it. She wrote:

...The respectful thing to do for a fine animal is to give it relief and the vet carefully killed the llama. The other llama will benefit from your attention more than ever. As I write this, I think about some of the conversations we have had. I am curious about whether you feel an emotional response to knowing that one of the llamas is dead...

Craig wrote back:

The pain of living can be quite difficult to bear at times, and that is especially true when one is physically encumbered/handicapped. As long as the killing is enacted for the good of the individual rather than to the perceived benefit (i.e. food, profit and/or even retribution in our criminal justice system through the death penalty) of others (society at large), it is justified. Thus, the killing of the llama meets such conditions, as the llama was in pain and the vet killed him/her to give him/her relief. While this might have profound effects on others as we recollect our memories with the llama, we must come to the realization that it was for the good of the animal and not put the well-being of ourselves before the well-being of any individual.

The main reason that I am coming to the farm is because it provides me with different experiences than where I live in Maryland. For example, if people decide to small talk while I am accomplishing various farm tasks, I can focus my attention on the work that I am completing and let people know that I am paying at least some attention to what they are saying (Whereas, over here, I do not have an excuse for failing to pay full attention to an individual.) I also avoid small talk by working without breaks and by not attending community meetings if I need time to myself. Moreover, upon coming back from completing farm chores, there are so many people that I can hide myself within a large crowd, which is often impossible at other places. Furthermore, I frequently feel as if I am needed at the farm, and I never truly get that feeling elsewhere...

Copying that piece triggers so many memories. I remember reading the part about the llama being put to sleep and knowing how much Craig was comparing it to himself. I remember thinking: if Craig could maintain himself at the farm, he might be able to eventually feel and connect better. I remember all our deepest wishes and hopes from that special moment.

Chapter Eight: Purpose and Community

After his first month at the farm, Craig wrote this letter to his Grandma Kay in Florida:

Thank you for taking the initiative to write to me. I am finding it difficult to engage in small talk (i.e. talking about the weather), but I do appreciate open contact.

You were very correct that I am busy here at the farm. It consists of many different work teams such as the kitchen, garden, forest and grounds, maintenance and farm teams. I am on the farm team, so I am frequently involved with cleaning cow, chicken and pig pens, as well as gathering hay, painting, rock picking, collecting eggs, etc. While these would not sound like fun tasks, I truly enjoy being productive and feeling a sense of accomplishment.

During the remainder of the day, there is always something to do. Poetry reading, discussion groups, town trips and sports are just some of the activities offered here.

Craig Climbed a Tree

The only day that I have a lot of free time is on Sunday because church trips dominate the day. Even then, I can go hiking or walk the llama.

How are you doing with the massage products? I hope I didn't overload you with products last time you requested some.

I would offer you a chance to come and visit me here, but I'm not sure whether you could occupy yourself while I am busy doing tasks and being involved in activities for almost all of the day. Tell me what you think.

Craig was always at his best when he had things to do all day. We were comforted to know that Craig was having good experiences and we wanted them to continue.

For weeks, Craig did not take breaks during the day and didn't eat meals with other people. His days were spent with the chickens—sorting eggs, cleaning out chicken poop, and listening to NPR on the radio. Much of his later interest in international relations and especially indigenous people stemmed from NPR and discussions around the farm community. Ken reminds me that Craig, with his remarkable perseverance, removed two feet of congealed chicken poop, and when we visited he was proud to show us the markings of where the poop had been.

Fran and Craig Wishnick

Slowly, with the encouragement of staff and guests, Craig began to have more conversations and joined the community at mealtime. Meals often included the children of staff members, an important normalizing experience for Craig. People with mental health challenges often isolate themselves, or are discouraged from joining in with family members for normal mealtime interactions. A major breakthrough for Craig occurred when he was sitting next to a little boy and actually began laughing with him and enjoying himself. Delighted with this development, the Admissions Director called to tell us about it.

Once a week, the farm had a community-wide meeting. At first, Craig sat outside the circle at the meetings and strongly disliked being praised. His face would turn beet red and he would sometimes walk out. Over time he 'allowed' himself to hear people say good things about him and very occasionally he did the same for others. Accepting and giving praise is a life-skill he developed there.

Craig also benefitted from hearing about other people's problems and coping skills during group therapy sessions.

During the summer and early fall, Craig loved playing baseball, as well as swimming and hiking. Baseball at the farm was different than what he had previously experienced. People didn't make fun of him—they encouraged him, and their kind, congenial attitude allowed him to feel better and enjoy himself.

Although his grandma didn't get to visit, we did, for family weekends and other times. Ken remembers family weekend so well. One time, Ken was helping out on the farming team with Craig and noticed a hand saw was being used when a power saw was available close-by. He mentioned it to Joe, a staff member not much older than Craig. Joe replied, "Ken, we learn to work with what we have." Ken heard those words loud and clear, as it pertained to Craig and to us all. Many years later, Ken still thinks about that simple but critical life lesson.

Meanwhile, Craig called or e-mailed us every few days, usually to ask about how to handle a situation at the farm, or when worried about what he was going to do next after he left the farm. We vigorously deflected those questions and concerns, telling him to talk to the clinical and other farm staff. Each farm guest had a clinical 'contact person' and Craig talked to his compassionate staff member extensively. If he thought he didn't get an answer or an answer that satisfied him, we were his fallback. Remember, Craig was black-and-white in his thinking, and when he asked a question, he could not understand or accept an equivocal answer like, "We'll see," or "Maybe you could." In an e-mail, Craig wrote:

When people use conditional tenses (instead of absolutes), I am absolutely lost as to what their message is (are they speaking English????) Examples: a) This may be seen as...b) This may be considered...c) Might want to think about or consider...d) Some may see this as...e) This doesn't mean that everyone believes....f) Might want to reconsider...g) Not everybody is going to agree...h) This could lead other people to believe that...

Craig couldn't understand why people talk like that!

One series of calls and e-mails were about Craig obtaining a driver's license. Ken and I had talked about this extensively. On one hand, we couldn't quite imagine Craig could ever drive because of his visual and perceptive problems, his inability to deal with unexpected situations, and his depression. On the other, we didn't want to over-protect him. We tried hard to allow him to reach his full potential. Ken and I agreed Craig could go for his driver's license, but would be driving many hours with us before, and if, we would ever let him have use of the car. The farm was able to arrange for driving lessons and eventually, with difficulty, Craig obtained his driver's license.

Craig Climbed a Tree

As the summer and early fall passed, Craig continued to be antsy about what he was going to do next. The flow of people through the farm during the warm months and the many activities had slowed as the seasons changed. We, as "good parents," had previously let Craig know our beliefs about how important college was, and those conversations became re-occurring thoughts for him. While he was at the farm, we tried to explain how college could be delayed for as long as needed and that would be fine, but it wasn't acceptable to him. Because Craig was literal in his thinking, he repeated to us verbatim the things we had said in the past. Boy, were we sorry we had emphasized college so much, as normal as it had seemed at the time!

There was a significant academic scholarship awaiting him at college too, and Craig knew it would only be held for a year. He kept asking us how much we were paying for him to be at the farm, how much we would need to pay for the step-down program, and what the anticipated college expenses would be. As concerned as we were about our financial resources, we didn't want the decision to be determined solely by money, but rather on what would be best for Craig. However, Craig couldn't and wouldn't allow the conversation to be based on more than finances and his own reports of his readiness.

Fran and Craig Wishnick

We asked ourselves: Should we insist that Craig remain at the farm even though he wanted to leave? Was Craig making decisions that were inappropriate for him? Ultimately, we realized:

- ☐ Since the farm was a purely voluntary program, we couldn't insist that Craig stay against his will.
- ☐ As when Craig was a child and was "ready to go" after an activity, nothing could stop him.
- ☐ Maybe Craig knew what was best for himself, and it *was* time to begin college.
- ☐ Ultimately, our finances were limited, and although we didn't tell Craig, we knew we couldn't continue to support his treatment. In other words, though we didn't in any way want to pressure Craig, the reality was that choices needed to be made.

After a great deal of tossing and turning, we decided to have yet another neuro-psychological evaluation done, while Craig was still at the farm, in order get information for us, as well as for any college he might attend. The testing was done by an independent practitioner who communicated with the farm. They said there had been:

...a huge change for the better....more willing to engage in small talk, to remain at meals and talk to others instead of rushing off, and to engage with others in

sporting activities. He smiles more, laughs more
appropriately, and less rigid about what is "useful and not
useful...

Craig divided the world into "useful" and "not
useful" and could be quite rigidly devaluing about the "not
useful." The examiner then described Craig's cooperation
during the testing:

...He came willingly to the testing room and,
throughout the seven-hour long evaluation, showed no
signs of wavering in his professed commitment to complete
the testing in one sitting. While Craig could not be
described as polite, neither was he ever rude or devaluing
(to me). Instead, his demeanor was straight forward and
business like, and he attacked the various testing
procedures with an obvious desire to be precise and
efficient. He took pleasure in getting something right, and
became obviously frustrated when he knew he had gotten
something wrong. However, his frustration never boiled
over to anger and tantrum. On the other hand, he would
sometimes obsess over a perceived error to the extent that it
interfered with his problem-solving on subsequent tasks.

While I've held back from extensively quoting
medical reports, the next few paragraphs are the
exception:

Fran and Craig Wishnick

Craig gave fifteen responses to the Rorschach Inkblot Test which is within normal limits. However, he was unable perform a substantial part of the inquiry...His first response to card one was "A bat." When asked to locate and describe it, he said, "Can you give me an example of how someone would describe something." At first, I thought he was being guarded and defensive. However, I eventually realized that, while he could state an impression of an ambiguous stimuli (inkblots are nothing in particular), he struggled to describe something that did not have the specific form or detail of an actual object in his external environment....as was evident in his comment at the end of the test: "This was really tortuous."

Craig prefers a world that is black and white, that is certain, concrete, not ambiguous. Usually, he would describe the actual physical features of the blot as opposed to a description of what he imagined it to be. However, there were times when his descriptions did become somewhat abstract. For example, on card ten, he initially resisted saying anything at all: "I feel like those people in Florida staring at a butterfly ballot. I don't see anything in this one." Then, he suddenly said, "An attack on Iraq...an Israeli's revenge for a Palestinian attack because of the weapon here {points}...this is coming out fast. It's hard to explain why." There were a few other instances where

Craig was able to be imaginative – to envision something that wasn't really there – that suggested that at times, and in small ways, he could get beyond the concrete to the abstract.

Because of Craig's anomalous performance on the Rorschach, it could not be scored statistically. On the other hand, I was able to form a number of clinical impressions... many of Craig's original perceptions were quite idiosyncratic, suggesting that he does not view the world in conventional ways. Also, there were indications of a morbid and somatic preoccupation.... that signal a depression. While there was little evidence that Craig lacked current adequate behavioral controls, there were indications of substantial angry, depressive, poorly modulated affect (emotions) that he worked hard at trying to keep from awareness. In other words, he preferred to remain detached from his emotional world, which required that he exert much energy in preventing distressing emotions from entering his awareness. This helps to explain why Craig can sometimes verbalize that he is suicidal or depressed (as though it was part of a personal theory or philosophy) while displaying affect which is incongruous to what he is saying (e.g. laughing or seeming lighthearted while speaking about depression and suicide). His emotions and his thoughts do not connect...

Reading this now, I believe the examiner was completely correct in his description of Craig's emotional world, his difficulty with abstract concepts, and how he did not view the world in conventional ways. Those serious difficulties persisted throughout his life.

Ultimately, given Craig's desire to begin college, the examiner recommended that the family be very involved in helping him make the college transition, including:

> ...frequent phone calls and visits, allowing him to return home on weekends and specific help with studies. It may even include brief periods of time spent "living" near the college.

The examiner recommended specific steps to take with the college for Craig's depression and cognitive limitations and also recommended that Craig have his own dormitory room, be assigned a school mentor who is not a peer, avoid courses that require visual/spatial skills, and that:

> Craig's teachers should understand that he is actually quite bright and capable of doing college work, but that his often rigid, detail-oriented cognitive style can be an obstacle to his thinking in that fluid, flexible, abstract style often required for some courses (such as literature).

The report concluded that Craig was:

...smart and persistent and, as has been shown at the farm, able to make improvements in his ability to socialize and inhibit impulsive behavior. However, he cannot fulfill his academic capability outside of much family support and a structured academic setting attuned to his vulnerability to stress, anxiety, and depression. He certainly deserves an opportunity to attend college and he has the potential to succeed. However, his family and his college will need to take the measures outlined to help engender this success.

We gave Craig an opportunity to read this report. He disagreed with a few items, but reaffirmed his desire to attend college. With that, and a day spent at the college meeting with school and vocational rehabilitation staff, Craig left the farm to begin his college career. However, this was not the end of his experience with the farm community.

Chapter Nine: Small Talk

Just prior to Craig beginning college, I met with their Student Services Office and other staff, as well as a state Vocational Rehabilitation Agency representative. I had requested the meeting in order to fully inform them about Craig's disabilities and his special needs in a college environment. Services offered by the school's disability office were explained. I then met with the Dean of First Year Students. Craig and I had previously toured the campus and had met the Dean at that time. It was clear she was going to do everything possible to help him succeed, and I think Craig understood and accepted their connection.

Ken and I remember move-in day very well. Craig's room was a fourth floor walk-up and he had boxes of stuff. Despite Ken's attempts to show him, Craig didn't know how to pack, and he also underestimated how difficult it would be to carry the boxes. Objects fell out of his hands and boxes as we went up the steep stairs. We were out of breath by the third round. Craig never understood how his high level of physical stamina, when he wanted to accomplish something, was different than ours. We tried to breathe, rest, and remain calm in the midst of our sweating and effort, and his—and admittedly our—general anxiety about this big transition.

Craig's priority was to immediately fill the room with good smells and soft objects, consistent with his sensitivities to smell and touch. Ken helped him with the mechanical stuff—setting up the television, light fixtures, etc. Craig had never inserted a light bulb before, and was actually frightened at the thought. I tried to help him unpack but he wanted to do it himself, so I sat there trying to keep the emotional climate even. After many hours, we left. We didn't know what to expect next.

Craig had turned down our offer of a cell phone, so we gave him a phone card and a phone in his room. During the first few days, he called us many times about people drinking on his floor, interactions he had, and whether he had said or done the "right" thing. However, Craig couldn't tolerate being on a "drinking floor," and after a week or so he moved downstairs to a floor that was set aside for non-users.

Fran and Craig Wishnick

Ken and I went on a short vacation to Nevada. At the Las Vegas airport, I turned on my cell phone in the luggage pick-up area. Within minutes, Craig called. Ken's face turned white. He knew it was possible we'd have to turn around and go home, or to the college. We vividly recall hearing Craig say this was "a bad time for us to be away"—as if there was any time that was good! Time has diminished my memory of exactly what that particular crisis involved, but I remember telling him to talk to the Dean, and that we'd be back in a few days. We needed that vacation so very badly.

I waited a day, then called Craig. The situation he had called about was under control, but a new one had emerged. He had enrolled in two short winter-session courses: Ethics and Film, and Badminton. Movies were usually tricky for Craig, because most involved non-literal material, but he was very interested in ethics. However, two of the films were in that non-literal, somewhat abstract category. We discussed this and I tried to help him with his anxiety.

Craig, with his fearsome determination, researched the movies on-line, and once he understood the plots, he was able to watch the movies. He received an A in that course.

Craig Climbed a Tree

During the spring term, Craig took less than a full load and aced those classes as well—except for Volleyball. He played the game well but couldn't comprehend the visual-spatial diagrams that were taught. His lack of understanding, his instructor's puzzlement about him, and his grade bothered him tremendously. We did everything possible to reassure Craig that his only C was in a half-credit course and how ultimately, it didn't matter. He kept trying to get us to talk with the instructor but we didn't think it was appropriate. Eventually, he calmed down.

Each time that a professor handed out a course outline at the beginning of the term, Craig studied it intently and often had many more questions than professors were willing to entertain at the time. Craig could only feel comfortable when he understood the nature of assignments completely and he felt compelled to understand all of them right away. Part of the reason was there were many days that Craig was depressed and anxious he was unable to do assignments. He knew his limitations all too well, so he often did assignments in advance. A few professors believed he did not belong in college, and openly said it to him. When that occurred, Craig felt it keenly and it consumed him. Nonetheless, the vast majority of professors came to understand Craig and his needs, and in those classes he not only excelled but contributed greatly to discussions with his unusual questions and world-view.

Other problems arose. Unlike his experiences at the farm community, groups of students in the cafeteria didn't necessarily welcome others at their table. Socializing was far from natural for Craig, especially when Craig saw much of it as "'small talk." He tried to find a way to sit with people because his experiences at the farm had taught him that he wanted to connect with his peers. The College Dean and others helped, but, rightly or wrongly, Craig focused intently on his "mistakes," and couldn't tolerate the social environment. Also, as a long-time vegetarian, and a picky one at that, he had difficulties finding food to eat in the cafeteria. He ended up eating out a lot, then feeling upset about the cost and the separation from other college students. Craig frequently called us asking for advice and solutions, and was distressed when we didn't know what to say.

I visited the college many times that first semester, often staying for several days. Sometimes I met with the Student Services Office or the College Dean; other times I just sat with Craig, and tried to interpret certain aspects of human behavior that confused him. Craig's questions about life and socialization often confounded even me. I spent many a night thinking in ways I had never thought before.

Craig asked about returning to the farm for the spring break. The First Year Student Dean at the time clearly remembers seeing Craig leave the college pretty worn down, and returning with his head up, offering more eye contact. This was after a week or so of the farm. I don't mean to describe the farm as ideal, and Craig wouldn't have. But it worked for him, in the most significant ways.

In fact, Craig decided that he wanted to return to the farm for the summer, before beginning a full college year in the fall. We remember he specifically said how he wanted to work on himself, and on socializing. Despite the expense, it was more than fine with us. Lindsay was graduating from college, and Craig felt he could not tolerate the graduation festivities, so we brought him to the farm for the summer, and set out for Lindsay's graduation.

Sometime later, Craig wrote another letter to Grandma Kay in Florida:

Please don't take it personally if/when I don't respond to your letters. I am spending quite a bit of time at the farm working on myself and analyzing how I respond to things that stress me out (i.e. small talk, others having authority over me). ...I have grown to understand my personality extremely well. Analyzing these letters, it seems that they are substantially based on small talk and thus, I try to avoid them as much as possible. However, it's good to have open dialogue with family and relatives. This leaves me puzzled about how to best approach the situation.

Here's a general overview of what my routine is at the farm. I work on the farm team Monday through Friday, 6 hours a day, completing various chores such as cleaning cow and pig poop, collecting and cleaning chicken eggs, cleaning the cheese room, gathering animals that escape and feeding the animals bread, grain and hay. In the summer, there [are] activities afterwards such as volleyball, softball, basketball and tennis (as well as trips to pick fresh fruit!) ... there have been intriguing trips lately to conversation groups about the possible war on Iraq and what we can do as citizens to avoid it. I also work at their store on Saturday and Sunday, seven hours a day, mostly cleaning dishes and clearing tables. The staff members at the store are really helpful in encouraging me and thanking me for how hard I worked...It is hard to explain the environment here in a letter!

You've probably heard from my parents that I'm interested in pursuing a career in International Relations without public speaking or fully being a translator. I am really hoping such a career exists. Since this uncertainty makes me uncomfortable, I try not to think too far into the future. Nevertheless, it's definitely safe to say that I'm excited about the college educational experience.

Chapter 10: Knockers and Nuances

Prolonged, dreary breaks have slowed the writing of this chapter. It is heartbreaking for me to think about a time in Craig's life when he had hopes and dreams. How, if he could just master the intellectual material, get excellent grades, and figure out some social cues, he would have a "good life." How we wished for that good life! I can hear his hopeful voice even now.

Good periods in college emerged when he was able to visualize a path for himself. We often bolstered his dreams when he felt deflated, anxious, and depressed which happened with much more frequency and intensity than for a typical college student. His learning disabilities and different learning style revealed themselves in many of Craig's classes. Nevertheless, his college years were relatively stable, with extended good times and increased confidence. We are very grateful that he had these experiences.

Craig Climbed a Tree

Ever since middle school, Craig adored Spanish language, culture, and music. He stayed with Spanish throughout high school and college. Silvio Rodriquez, a leftist Cuban folk music singer, was one of his favorites. Craig was energized by the pulse and cadence of the Spanish language. Their culture's diversity and energy was a source of enjoyment to him and he frequently told us he wanted to live in a non-English- speaking area.

Unfortunately, the same problems he had with non-literal English language emerged in his academic college study of Spanish. Once he reached the point of classes in Spanish literature or film, his problems with interpretation hindered him. At times Craig used an interesting technique which I believe he developed for himself. When available, Craig would get notes that described the characters then equate each character to someone he knew personally. Using that rather clumsy method, he then read the actual story. He did this for both English and Spanish classes. The amount of work that went into his reading was incredible. Sometimes he had to ask the deans and disability office to intervene, for extra time. Nevertheless, with assistance, persistence and ingenuity, he completed enough classes to have a Spanish minor.

Fran and Craig Wishnick

Craig also received college credit for Spanish study in San Miguel de Allende, Mexico. I traveled there with him and stayed in a bed and breakfast for a few days while he stayed with a host family, ultimately for several weeks, and studied at a Spanish-speaking school during the day. When we first got off the plane in Guanajuato, Mexico, Craig smiled broadly because he understood the spoken Spanish all around us and I didn't. He was in his element. I hold those smiles so dearly in my memory.

Although all of us would have wished it so, Craig's disabilities didn't disappear just because he was in another country. The sun came up and Craig was still Craig. For example, after the taxi-bus dropped me off at the San Miguel bed and breakfast, it took him to his host family's home. About an hour later he returned to my place. He couldn't find a doorbell or a knocker on the host family's door. Together, we walked back there. The knocker was much higher up on the door; according to Craig, it just wasn't where it was supposed to be. It was black-and-white thinking, once again.

Nonetheless, Craig loved the people, language and culture of San Miguel. He explored on foot and by public transit, by himself, without fear. He found places that smelled wonderful to him; he found hidden parks and trails. He took buses to explore the outskirts and always reported back to us about his discoveries and stresses. Were we nervous that he was by himself exploring a foreign world? Yes! Would we have stopped him? No. We wanted Craig to experience life, find some peace and joy, and we're glad we allowed him to have that opportunity.

Craig's junior year was spent at another college. Their course selections excited him and he wanted to try a new college environment. It worked and it didn't. With some accommodations he completed his courses, but life outside the classroom was always stressful for him. The administration there became all too aware of him because of his unusual behaviors. We fielded daily calls and made a number of trips to help.

Back at his original college for his senior year, Craig majored in political science, with a concentration in international relations. Some have commented how ironic it is that Craig was intensely interested in international relations, when he had such difficulties with interpersonal relationships. Thinking philosophically, at a remove from his personal interactions, Craig could explore nuances and details. He spent a lot of time talking with his advisor, who grew to admire him and his work, although at first she was startled by Craig's intense questions and different approach to learning.

Fran and Craig Wishnick

Long before his senior year, Craig became fascinated with the indigenous people of central and south America and decided to do his thesis on the topic, "Can Incorporation of Indigenous Peoples Coexist with Promoting Human Rights: Case Studies in Chile and the Ecuadorean Amazon." From his sophomore year onward, Craig prepared for his thesis and had boxes full of reference materials that are still closeted at our house. He was also fascinated by President's George W. Bush's use of the pre-emption doctrine for the war in Iraq.

I'll describe now what Craig thought, because this was of great interest to him beyond his academic studies and it shows his logical thinking.

Bush's pre-emption doctrine asserted that, when necessary, the United States would act preemptively in exercising an inherent right of self-defense. There were disagreements at that time about this doctrine. Craig wrote of his recollections of a chat that he had with his professor:

> *Professor: Sure you could use the topic of containment and deterrence in order to show the radical change in policy the preemption doctrine, which enables the President to destroy threats before they exist.*
>
> *Craig: This is not a radical change. The Carter doctrine said the U.S. would interfere when oil...*

Professor: But this is a totally new doctrine giving the President much more...

Craig: If you consider the history of overthrowing governments like Salvador Allende ...

Professor: But that was a covert action that people like me are trying to stop...

Craig: Yes, but since they took place when there was really no threat, and then when you look at the September 11th attacks, it is only natural that the President would try to legalize such action.

Professor: Yes, unfortunately that is true, but it is still a huge change from our past doctrines.

Craig wanted the world to make sense, and he tried to understand human thought and behavior. On one college break, Craig was home with us and in good spirits. In a memorable talk with Ken, he asked what Ken was like when he was in college, and they talked about college-aged Ken's values. "Why did you change? Why did you become a capitalist?" Craig asked. Long after Craig went to sleep, Ken was thinking about that one! Ken is usually not spontaneous, but that evening he asked me if we should consider selling our house and most of our possessions and volunteering at a residential mental health community, like the place that had so greatly helped

Craig. I was flabbergasted, but the more I thought about it, it made sense for us.

So we did it. The farm didn't have volunteer spots at that time, but another wonderful residential mental health community in the south did. We packed up and moved there, then, a year later, to the farm in New England that had helped our son. Craig was still in college throughout this time.

Occasionally, Craig had college experiences that sounded normal for his age. Once, he took the train into the city for the first time, and wrote:

...My trip to NY was great, and I found another person to walk around with who seemed a lot like Norris at the farm and mostly did shopping but also explored Greenwich Village, Times Square, Carnegie Hall etc. The metro system was so confusing but a good experience!

So now I come back to the realization that I'm tied down with a bunch of assignments that are due soon, and I am not here to have fun. Oh well.

During Craig's summer at the farm before college, he became friends with a volunteer there -I'll call her Tina- who was the same age as Craig. The friendship was very important to Craig and he tried to hold onto it even when both he and she were back at their respective colleges. At one point during a college break, Craig visited with Tina. After a year or so, Craig mournfully told us that they were no longer communicating. I found this e-mail to her in a box of correspondence that he had saved:

. .. Essentially what happens is that I realize that I am not in my best mood for whatever reason and feel a strong need to relate my feelings and imperfections to someone, which in this case is to you. But then I realize as we begin a conversation that it is difficult for you to help me process my negative thoughts and that you would prefer to enjoy the natural environmental surroundings or odd coincidences in life, which I think is really cool but it does not always fit in with my emotional state. I then get paranoid that I am bringing your mood down and drawing you away from enjoying yourself, which makes me try to "force" a connection by asking you if you've ever dealt with the feelings I have or how you are able to stay so positive. At this point, I notice that you are extremely uncomfortable, so I feel that I am not being a good friend by focusing on my inner feelings. You probably get the picture by now. It is a strange cycle of paranoia because you seem so stable whereas I go through times where I really struggle. I know that in the past, your positive energy was definitely a contributing factor in helping me feel better at the farm, and I hope to benefit more in the

future from that energy, but I am not always ready to embrace it.

As Craig see-sawed with his daily emotions and desire for friendships, we heard and saw a pattern. When he found a friendly person and wanted to connect, inevitably he would end up disclosing his depressive and anxious feelings and feel uncomfortable about having done so. Then he would compensate for his discomfort by attempting to get the other person to reveal their emotions to him—and he did so much too early and intensely in the "friendship." Sooner rather than later, either Craig or the other person would pull away.

Craig questioned us extensively about how friendships work and attempted to write detailed instructions for himself:

> *...my realization is that since people are quite stressed out in their own lives and have enough serious things to be concerned/ worried about, they are always looking to befriend people who they perceive are at a lower stress level than them. If they perceive this other person to be at a higher stress level than them, this does not necessarily stop a friendship from being formed but it is a major setback in terms of what they are looking for. So the key is to make people perceive you're not as stressed out as you are and to joke around/have fun/talk in a playful way as much as*

possible until they form a friendship, which makes each other feel comfortable and confident that their stress levels are relatively low and won't be a burden. Once a deep friendship is formed and both people feel comfortable enough with each other, then it is more acceptable to show vulnerabilities etc. because they already understand each other well enough that they can't hide or fake things as easily.

Another day, when he was more isolated, he wrote:

In an alternative scenario, one can rely on him/herself for predictable behavior, be it for happiness, sadness or both. He/she can still socialize with others but not be forced to speak in uncomfortable circumstances, as friendships require. These interactions, in turn, will help one to further understand him/herself and the human condition while not putting oneself through an emotional roller-coaster —an often illogical one to say the least.

I am constantly analyzing whether I'm "getting my money's worth" from other people. Investing in them requires enough returns for you to make a living.

Chapter 11: Too Good

Between Craig's junior and senior year, he participated in a Spanish immersion program in Quetzaltenango, Guatemala. The program wasn't connected with his college; Craig had researched and found the opportunity himself. As in San Miguel, in Quetzaltenango (locals call the city Xela for short, pronounced shell-ah), he lived with a host family and attended classes. Craig was thrilled that he had an opportunity to learn some of the indigenous Mayan language, called Q'equchi.

Xela is over 7,000 feet above sea level and Craig enjoyed exploring the unique city and its environs. Sometimes he went on organized hikes with the program, but mostly he explored the area himself and traversed some rugged terrain. We were pretty worried about him during his risky trips and especially about his difficulties in relationships. For example, once he called to say that the Guatemalan host family's mother was angry at him, although he wasn't sure why. He thought he might get kicked out, but fortunately he was able to stay there the full three weeks.

One call from Craig in Guatemala made us laugh and cry. He was entranced by the look of the young Mayan women, and apparently one time, on a bus, he spoke to a woman who asked him if he wanted to marry her. The thing was, Craig only partially saw this as humorous. He understood on some level that it was not about him, but he wanted it to be, and kept asking us if he should give her his money or go to her house. We told him no. He listened, thank goodness.

When Craig returned to his college for his senior year, he again immersed himself in his thesis. He had been preparing for this for several years, and his ultimate reference list topped 100 books and materials. He felt confident and it showed—his thesis was well-constructed. This, plus his efforts in other classes, resulted in Craig being the recipient of the department's political science award. In addition, he was accepted into Pi Sigma Alpha, the national political science honor society.

We've lost most of the e-mails during Craig's college years. However, in a saved one, Craig told of his thoughts du jour:

Fran and Craig Wishnick

I believe that if Socrates were living today, he ...would not be popular socially, even with professors. College students and professors really enjoy learning/teaching about these concepts but then want a private life that is separate from this in which they small talk and do not open their eyes to the fact that they are excluding other people...People can be good if they open their eyes (as typically occurs at the Farm), but it is often easier to do what is natural for them...

Back to working on socialization, my colds, as you probably know, always make me brutally honest and turn me back to my roots rather than improvements. So I was deeply ingrained in my thoughts when I ran into Vicky, who gave me her well written senior thesis last year.... I was so dizzy when she was speaking and so into my thoughts that all I could do was look at her and say "yeah, that's true." ...These are the types of interactions that I need to be able to "master" at any time regardless of how I am feeling if I want to begin to make friends.

Craig was extremely anxious about, and constantly questioning, what he would and could do, post-graduation. International relations, and especially working with indigenous people, were his interests, but he had no idea how to turn them into a career. especially with his limitations, of which he was all too aware. He was afraid and incapable of networking, but he went to the college's career office and also met with the state vocational rehabilitation people in Maryland. Basically, he was told to use computer resources to look up possibilities and then...what? Write letters.

Just like his fellow students, he did. Ironically and significantly, Craig wanted to be as independent as possible, and didn't want us, his parents, to use our contacts and resources on his behalf.

His anxiety, feelings of social isolation and depression were worsening. He called us about incontrollable twitching, and obsessive compulsive behaviors. In the midst of the second semester of his senior year, he needed to come home. He was not in good shape, just three credits short of graduation.

At first, we worked with Craig to see coming home as an opportunity to get some more intensive therapy around his social isolation, depression, and other issues. It was also time for us to leave the farm, so we decided to move to upstate New York, where we believed Craig could get the therapy he needed. (We had located a therapist well-versed in Asperger's.) This was at Craig's request. He articulated his lack of understanding of social cues as a primary source of his anxiety and depression. After a few meetings with him, the therapist related her concerns to me about his perception that the world was overwhelming, how every feeling he had was amplified '100 times', how his sensitivity and sensory issues were intense. She provided an example where Craig said that whenever someone around him yawned, it felt like it was "burning his face." She went on to say that she was "worried that he's shutting down." Craig always struggled with transitions and the transition from a structured college environment to his unpredictable life and future was problematic.

All that was roiling him internally finally resulted in a psychiatric hospitalization. The hospital's medical team told us we needed to back off and let Craig face his struggles more independently, given his age. With Craig's suddenly aggressive behavior toward us (a verbal threat, and the only time in his life where this type of behavior occurred), we should not let him come home to our house after the hospitalization. With misgivings, but not knowing what to do, we followed the medical team's directions.

The results were awful. The hospital discharged Craig to a motel, and a few days later, he attempted a drug overdose that resulted in a more serious and lengthy hospitalization, including an overnight stay in intensive care, where, he told me afterwards, a kind nurse said to him, "You're too young and good for this. I don't want to see you again here."

A few weeks later, he wrote this note to his former college dean:

I haven't been ignoring you – I just got out of the hospital two weeks ago after being there off and on for almost the entire summer. I was so depressed at one point that I dramatically overdosed on medications and somehow managed to call 911 about 9 hours after the overdose. But I'm somewhat better now because I have the structure of a day program three times a week which involves basic group sessions and provides a psychiatrist and therapist in exchange for attending. The program is good, but it's ironic that I miss the hospital because I developed deeper connections with people there because they were higher functioning and stuck there, so they might as well just socialize with whoever is there. I'm trying to finish my last three credits of college doing an independent studies project [about] the Rudolf Steiner Fellowship Community. It's an idealist community ...based on Rudolf Steiner's theories of spirituality and connecting with others. I'll be going there soon to visit so that should provide some relief from my isolation and feelings of hopelessness...

Fran and Craig Wishnick

When he returned from the Steiner community, he wrote a thorough report on his interviews with community members and the Steiner philosophy. For housing, he rented a room in a house near us. Meanwhile, his ulcerative colitis had flared up in the hospital, so he was dealing with physical pain as well as emotional distress. Minute-to-minute, he was dealing with depression and anxiety, fear of the future, wanting to do something productive, struggles with interpersonal relationships living in someone else's house and managing his medical problems and appointments. We were taking his calls and e-mails daily, taking him places and trying to help him sort things out. He was still furious at us for our perceived "lies" when he was a child and because we didn't have all the answers he wanted. The wedding vow, "for better or worse, in sickness..." applied in our attempts to help our profoundly disabled son, but our commitment to him left us isolated, uncertain and worried all the time. All the time. Here's an example of a not-atypical time:

I wake up at 2 a.m. hearing noises. I go downstairs and find Craig, who had been asleep on the couch, eating, or on the computer; he couldn't fall back asleep.

If he was at his house—a rented room in someone's home— there would be a call, first thing in the morning, about something Craig had stressed about during the night, or something we failed to fully answer the day before.

If we missed the call and tried to return it, it went to messages, and maybe he went back to sleep. Or maybe not. Since we were his only "responders," if we picked up the call, it set the stage for an entire day of responding to his needs. Of worry and self-doubt, for us.

Around this time-frame, Craig learned that Mel, a former guest at the farm, for whom Craig had a non-romantic affinity, had died from a physical ailment. He obtained her Mom's e-mail and wrote:

I keep thinking of Mel and just how grateful I am with how she relaxed me when I interacted with her. At the same time, I feel angry that we were never able to meet again...My mother tells me this is a normal feeling though. I have been cuddling with my dog a lot and walking her around, which helps quite a bit. ...I just want to see how you're doing now. I haven't been too good...but I think I'm starting to improve. I really feel that Mel is still present in my life, even though I really want to see her in physical reality. I'm really not used to these types of feelings because with my Asperger's Syndrome, I almost always think about what is here and in front of me in my everyday life vs.

missing people and especially with missing someone who isn't alive at least in physical form. I hope this makes sense and isn't too much theorizing...feel free to call me literally anytime (except in the middle of the night) if you need support or at least my attempt at being supportive.

Chapter 12: To Be Understood

Craig was twenty-three and seven months out of college when he wrote this morose description of his life:

> *Ulcerative colitis flairs up, I am supposedly in need of "counseling" for my social isolation and other issues, vocational placement agencies do not have placements in the type of work I need, my parents seem frustrated with my frequent phone calls, I am walking around buying items and doing physical workouts while not achieving a purpose that gives to others and society, diarrhea becomes out of control, there are no concrete steps I know of to change my situation. Is there any reason I have for hopefulness or that things will work out in the long term? I listen to music, take a shower and then a nap, hoping that I will awaken as a different person with new ideas. I need intellectual stimulation. I am angry at people for ending possibly long-term friendships with me, bleeding in my bowel movements has increased, what am I supposed to do*

until I fall asleep? Housing placement and low spending budget are of concern. I encounter a bad smell in the living room which worsens my mood. I have no reliable friends or people to talk to who understand. The doctor for my ulcerative colitis cannot see me until several weeks from now. I call my parents again and they seem agitated that I called again and practically beg for quiet time. Is living in a hospital or prison really different from these conditions? Where is everybody – nobody's on the streets except people walking as if they're drunk. At least I have access to my music and warm showers. I miss my dog and think about how she's getting older and I'm not able to benefit from her because I am living elsewhere. Were my parent's responses signs that they've had enough me or is this paranoia? I've gone 7 full months since I have finished college and what have I done other than pass time? Someone yawns as he passes by me, releasing a horrible odor. Counseling is so pointless because it only offers common senses solutions and over generalizes.

The themes in Craig's note were present throughout his young adult life. The ulcerative colitis flared every few months and involved considerable pain, diarrhea and bleeding. One of his prescribed colitis medications was Purinethol, a heavy-duty pill that wasn't meant to be taken long-term for his condition. Over time, several G.I.

doctors were concerned enough about long- term effects that they attempted to wean him off Purinethol, and onto a better-tolerated long-term medication, but his colon flared each time. In addition to the physical symptoms, such flare-ups meant Craig was confined to his room or our house, where he lay on the couch with Scruffy for days at a time, fueling his depression and anxieties. In itself, his overly-anxious state likely fueled those flare-ups. It was a vicious cycle that made us sick to our stomach to watch.

On a typical day in young adulthood, Craig e-mailed or called us often, when he wasn't at our house. If he didn't contact us for a few days, we knew there was a good chance that he was deteriorating. Calls and e-mails were about issues like losing an "important" coupon, being in an anxious state about how to deal with something that just happened or was anticipated, or telling us he was borderline about going to the hospital emergency room, due to his depression. Frequently, he wanted us to pick him up and bring him back to our house, so he could be with Scruffy to calm himself.

It was unclear to us how to respond to his needs and demands, and so frustrating. On one hand, he was a young adult with few supports. On the other, we were finding our lives too intertwined with his, and knew it was detrimental to both him and us. Within the space of any given day, Craig would want to be independent, then something would happen and he fell back onto dependency.

We were just plain exhausted. All too often, we wanted someone else to take responsibility for helping him. We felt ourselves slipping. We simply didn't know how to be good parents for Craig. It's hard to admit, but we had feelings of wishing he would go away—a not-uncommon emotion for family members of individuals with chronic mental health issues, or developmental disability. Craig had both, and more. Those feelings didn't linger within us, because we loved him so very much. But when we had them, we were miserable, and now, as we think so often about him, it feels even worse.

People kept telling us to "be sure to take care of ourselves." I'm sure they meant well but how was that supposed to happen?

We observed Craig as he tried to understand the world and to be understood. He tried to understand the process of socially connecting, coping with his anxieties, obsessive thoughts and actions and depression. He tried to understand what he could do in life to be productive. Granted, his need to understand and be understood was different, problematic and significantly more intense than what most people need. His inner-directed thought pattern could be seen as narcissistic and over-thinking or rumination, however, whatever it might be called, he couldn't seem to banish this pattern of thought at will.

When Craig was twenty-three, he wrote:

I really have trouble figuring out why people 'fault' me when they are unable to figure out helpful advice for my situations. The pattern is below:

☐ *Response to me: Well here's a way to think more positively, try a coping mechanism such as walking or showering to better process, it won't be resolved at heightened stress levels.*

☐ *But I've tried that! I wish it worked but it hasn't*

☐ *Response to me: Have you really tried? Try harder. You're just being negative and rejecting whatever is said. Well, what do you want us to say – this is what's available – you expect miracles? This can be a way to challenge yourself – do something you don't think will help.*

I can't believe how oversimplified this is given that I work super hard with trying new things, changing myself and keeping my expectations low regarding advice or help they might give. Perhaps these responses are instead a way of expressing frustration with not being able to think of positive ideas to help me?

Craig tried, on his own, to make friends. His social awkwardness belied his age. He was too quick to judge other people's 'energy,' couldn't tolerate 'small talk' (although he worked on that over the years), and often revealed too much about his intense emotions, and expected other people to do the same. To find friends, he posted these ads on-line:

Hi – I'm new to the area and am searching for a good, quality friend. I am an intellectual and animal lover who is quiet and shy. Yet, I am really direct (a huge plus if you're direct too!) and can sometimes surprise people by wanting to discuss thoughts/feelings involving philosophies about life and challenges myself and others are facing (animals can be SO therapeutic for this, hence I would like to include my small and lovable Cocker Spaniel/Terrier dog if a find a friend who likes to go hiking or some fun outdoor activity.) I really enjoy talking about politics, so bonus points if you appreciate the humor in the Daily Show and Colbert Report (lol, those shows are so funny!) I am absolutely NOT looking to be around people who are really into smoking, drinking, drugs, flirting and sex, so please don't e-mail me if that's what you're looking for. Be well, and have a good day!

Hello – I'm looking for someone to casually chat with but whose conversations do not center around drinking, smoking, flirting, personal appearances, and that kind of stuff. I'm looking for someone who is a bit "deeper" than that but does not somehow believe that their ideas are "superior" to those of others. A bit confusing? Yeah, it is for me too! Lol. But I'd very much like to find good quality friends ...Please e-mail me if this sounds interesting.

He received many spam-type messages, but no friendships emerged from these advertisements.

Chapter 13: Help me figure out where I am

...I just remembered listening to a ...tape that I used to listen to with my parents during car rides when my mom and I used to talk many years ago (we still talk – talk more and better!) that I occasionally made jokes about something funny and started laughing and being informal, and my mom and the few others I socialized with naturally took that as an opportunity to start sharing a similar thing or story that they found funny. However, when people started to say anything like, "That reminds me of ...", I got angry that they started comparing what I was saying to something they had in their mind, like they didn't care what I was saying and just had prefixed ideas and wanted to focus on those during the conversation rather than what I said. I now understand it's much more of a balancing act and that recognizing my thoughts, feelings and jokes and moving on is different and much more relaxed/fun oriented than asking a question in academia and getting a

straight and clear answer and then moving on to another point. However, possibly due to my Asperger's need for some predictability, abrupt change in topics are still a surprise to me when I'm really into telling something funny to me. So, with both discussing funny things and discussing possible negative emotions, is there an informal and socially appropriate way to let the other person know I want to focus on talking about myself or my thoughts at the moment and then would like to talk about anything they're interested in, in a way that comes across as wanting to be sensitive to my needs? Or is that too much to ask when it's an informal conversation and should only occasionally be used when there are actually negative emotions I need to process? Do others have this same need? If so, is there a way to tell, because I often interrupt when people pause for a few seconds during jokes or while talking...

For two-and-a-half years, Craig was enrolled in a mental health day treatment program, for adults who were seriously and persistently mentally ill. It offered groups for issues like anger management, assignment to a good, caring therapist, and an equally good and caring psychiatrist. Craig went to the groups only occasionally— his choice, since it was a voluntary program. He couldn't easily tolerate regular group participation for many reasons. The group subjects didn't meet his needs, and rightly or wrongly he felt that the people in the groups weren't like him. He couldn't tolerate the conversation, and felt he had things he needed to process that weren't being processed in the group. He didn't understand the body language. He met with his therapist and psychiatrist regularly, and called them often because he was symptomatic. Sometimes he came into the day program and reported suicidal thoughts or high anxiety, in such a way that the day program sent him to the hospital for evaluation. He also brought himself to the emergency room when he felt extremely depressed and stressed. He was hospitalized perhaps a half-dozen times during those years. Eventually, a hospital staff member told him that if he continued to be hospitalized so frequently, he would need to go to a state hospital. Craig reported this to us, in great distress, saying that they had removed his "safety place," an option for him when he couldn't handle life.

Around this time, Craig's psychiatrist at the day program came up with an idea that kept Craig out of the hospital, for the most part. He prescribed liquid Ativan, which was fast acting. This was important, because when Craig's anxiety level rose out of control, it sometimes rose so fast that Craig couldn't even attempt to use coping skills, or find someone to talk to. This medication was prescribed in small amounts as needed. Craig understood how to use it appropriately. I saw it work for him many times.

For our complex son, there were a multitude of issues, both mental and developmental. But he was categorized as primarily mental health, and put into that system of care. Craig was a person, not a silo! He needed help with his depression and anxiety issues, AND his lack of understanding of social norms. He was highly intelligent, despite his learning deficits. He often seemed much younger than his years, yet he mastered activities of daily living such as managing money and getting around with public transportation, and could analyze non-interpersonal problems within his many spheres of knowledge in a sophisticated manner that often blew us, and others, away. He had difficulty changing a light bulb, but he got excited by conferences he attended, with titles like "Prosperity and Inequality: Debates in India and China."

We applied for eligibility for Craig, under the state's developmental disability guidelines. We hoped beyond hope that he could get some special assistance in socialization. Since Craig desperately wanted to work, but had obstacles—understanding non-specific assignments, and job-related soft skills such as how to handle group and individual dynamics—we were hoping that he would qualify for services that would work on those areas with him.

We hit a brick wall. He didn't score *low enough* across the varied domains in the Adaptive Behavior Assessment System. In other words, although some of his skills in domains such as social were significantly low, he scored too high in functional academics and other areas, and thus did not qualify for developmental disability services. We appealed, but lost. During the appeal, I'll never forget one of the state officials turning to Craig as he said, "You need help, but not from us." Craig left the meeting frustrated, as did I.

Help! —but from where? Ken and I spent many sleepless nights going over real and imaginary possibilities. We wished we were wealthy so we could find the right mix of services for him without having to meet archaic system criteria. We knew then, and know now, that although Craig may have been unique, there are so many young adults with Asperger's who have aged out of school-based services, who need assistance to survive and, better yet, prosper. We were resourceful parents and still didn't have a clue where to turn for help.

We suggested to Craig that neuro-feedback might be an option, to relieve some of his stress. It was short-lived, but interesting. He had his brain mapped, and the doctor asked him if he had a brain injury as a child, since parts of his brain were operating extra fast, and some extra slow. I wasn't at this meeting so I can only relay what Craig told me. He went for a few more neuro-feedback treatments, but was hyper-conscious of how much it was costing us. Even though he felt some effects, they didn't last long, so Craig decided to stop treatment. While money was tight, we would have continued this treatment as long as it was needed, but Craig was an adult, and we needed to allow him to make his own decisions.

One expense for which we were glad to pay involved bus trips to Manhattan and the boroughs. Craig explored neighborhoods, parks, museums, and attended meet-up groups on mental health issues, such as depression. He had the skills to get around by walking or with public transit, and the resourcefulness to find free activities in the city. Occasionally we got a call from him asking us to Google-map him, so he could figure out where he was. His call would start out something like this:

Craig – Hi. So, I just crossed a bridge (by foot), I think it was the Brooklyn Bridge and now I'm in Brooklyn a few blocks from the bridge on a hill with lots of rocks. Can you help me figure out where I am?

Fran and Craig Wishnick

Each time we helped him locate his bearings, but it was both comical and scary to get those calls. Over time, he learned to figure it out himself, though he called us anyway and made us pretty nervous while he walked and processed his thoughts and location.

In retrospect, we must have gotten used to Craig being lost and figuring it out. One day, we got a series of calls from Craig and his mental health therapist. He got lost while hiking off-trail near our local area. His cell phone hadn't been charged in several days. We and his therapist wanted to keep the conversations short so his signal could be monitored, and he could be located. Park rangers, his therapist, the day program, and Ken and I were all involved. When Craig was told by a park ranger to just walk in a downhill direction, Craig said that he didn't see a hill. His therapist told him to just stay put. During those few hours, Ken and I felt calm. Considering all that we went through, with suicidal thoughts, hospitalizations, family dynamics and stress galore, this was just another day in "family life with Craig."

Chapter 14: Flush and Fit

During his first few years out of college, Craig went from one living environment to another. He was limited in how much rent he could pay by his SSI check of $761, and even more restricted by his need and desire for a non-partying, non-smoking environment. On several occasions, he found a place to live, but the housemate situation became untenable. He would question everything, and insist on consistency, or else misunderstand conversations. One time, he lived across the street from his landlord's family who, at first, said that he could stop by anytime. However, he took that literally, and stopped by several times in the evening, just as their family was relaxing for the night. Decidedly not what they meant by their invitation. He called that "inconsistency," and couldn't tolerate it, so for this and other reasons, we moved him out of there. We helped him move in and out of four apartments in three years, each time installing his futon, television, and boxes, answering his incessant questions about practical matters, like how to open a window, or how to work the stove.

Finally, Craig found a very good housing match with Elaine, a woman in her seventies. She was willing to put up with his foibles, even when he wrote notes reminding her to flush her own toilet when she used it at night! Elaine liked Craig, because he was direct, and insisted that she be the same. Since she actually wanted to make that change in herself, it was mutually beneficial. Elaine and Craig had some deep discussions as well, about international matters, and philosophy. However, even in that new, compatible environment, Craig's crippling social discomfort reared up, as he described in this e-mail to us:

So my landlady, Elaine, yesterday was having a conversation on the patio with one of her daughters, Clara, who's visiting from Florida. The door to the patio was open and I was smelling something strange outside, so I went outside while still holding onto one of my towels (need to say that detail here) and when I went out she kept offering to hang it up on the patio and also seemed apprehensive and almost looked like she was pretending to be a sumo-wrestler trying to push me away (in retrospect it's a funny perspective but at the time scary to me) When she started repeating "OK" in a tense/snappy voice a few times along with a sumo-wrestling attitude, I felt that she no longer cared about me because who would treat me that way for just walking outside (nothing wrong) if they liked me. Luckily, I have the ability in my mind to quickly sort through all archived experiences in only a second or two, and I then realized Elaine wanted a private conversation with Clara, so I acknowledged that and left. This type of experience where I heard an inconsistent response occurred a lot with my parents during childhood, at times due to my lack of information or understanding of situations and at other times my hypersensitivity to voice tones...makes me want to challenge them to see if they still care. The reaction still happens to this day, unless in this case I'm able to correct my feeling based on past experiences as I did in this example...

We stopped by on occasion to talk with Elaine, especially when Craig was in his room for days at a time because of his ulcerative colitis flare-ups, and/or his depression. Craig voluntarily hospitalized himself twice, and visited the emergency room several times while living at Elaine's house. He managed to get to the hospital by involving us, but not Elaine, thank goodness. Once, when he was feeling well, they went to a nearby state park—her to swim, him to hike—and she was concerned, because he didn't return when expected. She called us, as she did a couple of times when he returned to the house later than she expected. She didn't need to do all this. She cared.

Sometimes Craig e-mailed Elaine while they were in the same house. He had a cold, and was feeling paranoid about an interaction, when he wrote:

Hi Elaine-

So I think what really just happened is that you might not have wanted me to see you going through something in your room because if you were worried about my virus, you wouldn't have walked in my direction while I was talking! So I hope that you can be direct with me in the future...I know it's something that's difficult, but I'm still trying to understand social ambiguities and will often not understand situations as well as I think I did with this one. Hope you're well.

We were and are so grateful that Elaine put up with all of this and was in Craig's life.

During these few years, Craig desperately wanted a job, but his depression, anxiety, need for structure, social difficulties, ulcerative colitis, lack of experience, and the poor economy all hindered his efforts. For days at a time he couldn't have worked at a normal job, because his medical and psychological conditions kept him dysfunctional, lying in bed in his rented room or on our couch. On other days he managed to get himself together, and during those times, using his resourcefulness, he found volunteer opportunities that he called internships. It may be puzzling to people who never knew Craig to understand how he was able to control his social anxieties to the point of walking in, without an appointment, to ask about volunteer opportunities. All I can say is that one of Craig's great strengths and detriments was his determination. If he was feeling well enough, he could get himself together and present well, at least initially.

However, once he found an opportunity, he consistently ran into his two sets of problems – task processing, and having social relationships at work. Highly intelligent in certain areas, he needed to have structured work assignments, and he needed to ask questions until he fully understood the assignment, and how the work would be used. This was asking a lot, but it was the method he used, successfully, throughout college. If he had lingering questions, he felt that he didn't understand the assignment at all. It was all or nothing. Once, Craig attended a conference in Manhattan on food distribution to the needy, as prelude to a volunteer opportunity. It turned out that in order to volunteer, Craig and others had to "wing it" to some extent. Here's his explanation of why that didn't work out for him:

Fran and Craig Wishnick

The volunteer meeting for the Food Conference was very interesting, but it also made me realize how unable I am to contribute because all tasks require being able to spontaneously answer other people's questions without necessarily knowing the information. I've noticed in many cases that professionals have figured out ways to just give some wordy answer without directly answering the question, but that's just not me. I'm really not able to come up with that limited information – if I have limited information on anything, I just label it as not helpful (because limited information is never that helpful to me) and of course I can't verbalize what I know when I'm upset about not knowing more. I actually wish I didn't attend the conference because it only fueled my depression more, and makes me feel pretty useless, even though the conference was interesting.

There was also the social, what professionals call the "soft-skills" piece. The need to get along in individual and group relationships in a work setting. Several quotes from Craig's e-mails reveal his difficulties:

I care about how people are doing. I find it strange when I ask people who look tired if they're tired, including some of my co-workers as well as my psychiatrist today, as well as MANY people in the past, I get a quick snappy reaction saying, "I'm fine." As if I shouldn't be asking. Ironically, one of the co-workers that I asked this question to had just a few minutes prior to that told another co-worker how tired she was, but then again I know she doesn't enjoy my company on a friendship/relational level. I am in major need of knowing boundaries and who I should be asking this "tired question" to and how to predict when it might feel too personal for people...

And, in some quotes mentioning his volunteer work:

I need to change something at work and it's really hard, which is that I need to monitor how loud my voice is, especially when I'm talking to one staff member about other co-workers and how I'm trying to adjust to their specific styles. It's especially hard in this office because of the open floor though I hear they're probably making changes to the layout soon. I'm struggling with how high of a priority to place this as compared to focusing on doing good work and doing the pleasantries of hello, how was your weekend, small talk, mixing questions to people with informalities, etc. If I focused on doing everything right and then doing things outside of work correctly, I'm going to be completely burnt out. The answer is probably not nearly as clear cut as I'd like...

Here's another e-mail, funny but revealing, where Craig described his social discomfort:

Fran and Craig Wishnick

There seem to be so many restrictions on what I can say when someone at work, as happened today, says, "I'm working out because I need to be fit in time for my wedding." Everyone here, including me, knew about her wedding, so the only thing left is the weight issue. I tried to make a joke out of it by saying (it probably came out as muttering because I was nervous but laughing) "So I guess to hug everybody at the wedding, you need to be in good shape." I then tried to recover when I didn't get a laugh and tried to become an active listener by saying, "SO you just chose that as a day you'd like to be fit by", but that got a worse reaction. I'm so confused.

Chapter 15: Scream

It was confusing and overwhelming, for Craig and for us, for professionals in the field, and for family and friends. When people asked how "things were going," it was impossible to explain. Craig's mental state varied from day-to-day and within any given day. Our sense of hope and understanding varied as well. We wanted so badly for life to improve for him that we tried to find the positive every day, but too often we couldn't. We wanted and needed people to understand what he and we were going through, but didn't want to overwhelm them, or wear out their interest. More than anything, Ken and I wanted Craig to get the help that he needed, but all-too-frequently we were running on empty, without sufficient ideas, energy, and patience.

Craig's ulcerative colitis flared every few months, a source of immense concern and frustration. During a flare-up, Craig was dysfunctional. He stayed in bed for days, and cancelled doctor appointments and other activities. For days, even weeks at a time, he was out of circulation. Steroids were dangerous for him because they increased his mood problems. Yet, when the colitis was bad, steroids were prescribed. We knew the pattern. They would eventually calm the symptoms, but in the interim Craig's depression would skyrocket, so we needed to be close, monitor him constantly, and reassure him that it would pass.

When Craig saw a gastroenterologist, he was often given a recommendation that he reduce his high doses of steroids and other colitis medication, and try something new. That didn't work, and consequently he had some especially bad recurrences. We wanted Craig to believe in the medical profession, to believe he could advocate for himself and explain what had happened in the past, when he and they tried to lower his meds. Self-advocacy was a crucial part of his need to be as independent as possible. He even asked us to rehearse with him how to describe his symptoms. Unfortunately, doctors too often didn't listen to what Craig was telling them. Doctors can and do stigmatize a person who has a psychological impairment, and are frustrated when a patient cannot fairly represent what is happening to them physically. Craig was certainly highly anxious about body ailments, but he needed to be heard, not ignored.

I'll never forget the time Craig called his G.I. doctor multiple times to explain that the lowered medications were causing bleeding and painful symptoms. He wasn't being heard, and it frustrated him so much I had to intervene and insist that a new colonoscopy be scheduled. While Craig was still sedated after the procedure, the doctor came over to report to me that Craig's colon was severely inflamed, and that, "Craig didn't tell us how bad it was."

I don't know how I held back a scream. Perhaps I shouldn't have. Once again, high doses of steroids were prescribed and the depression intensified.

It was never easy. Once the flare-ups subsided, Craig tried to deal with his depressed mood, social difficulties and understanding of the world:

> ...*I am always trying to make sense of really complicated things, so I'm constantly categorizing things I see in life, trying to pick up patterns with what I see and better adjust my behavior to fit in society.* **I don't have the luxury that others have to try to remain from categorizing/judging.** *So when I verbalize that I am categorizing what others do or how they look, they feel judged and this stirs up protective feelings, and then in*

turn I am caught off guard and say things in a stronger way to defend myself because I didn't think I did something wrong (quite the opposite) which then makes others even more uncomfortable with me, etc. I really am not sure how to deal with this because I've made so many positive changes based on openly categorizing, analyzing etc. but then it makes me not an easy person to be around, for most people at least.

and

*...I noticed that it's totally social for people at work [a volunteer position] to say things around fellow employees like "fuck, I messed up on the fax, I'm such a loser" or "I was so fucking mad at them..." However, the employees viewed it as entirely different when someone was discussing her faith and how she's Christian and her husband is Jewish and from Israel and they're working with each other by attending each other's church and synagogue and how her children would likely grow up bi-religious. When I responded that, "There doesn't seem to be a pure religion these days...and I take a lot of comfort in that" the response was viewed by everyone in the room as socially inappropriate and one person snapped, "I'm glad **you're** comfortable about that" and quickly changed conversation. I don't think that what I said was nearly as inappropriate as the cursing, and yet that's how things*

are...I don't want to feel so frustrated and saddened by this but I do.

In a separate e-mail he wrote:

When people feel any negative feeling strongly, I call that "stress" because strong negative feelings are undoubtedly stressful to deal with. However, when I label it "stress" and ask if they're stressed, it seems like people perceive that as me asking if there's something wrong with them on a very personal level. That's not my intention, as stress is perfectly normal and can be a good thing, but maybe that's not what people believe? Is there a better way to go about asking which feels less like an affront?

Despite everything, Craig kept trying to figure out how to deal with his world. He continued to take bus trips to Manhattan and the boroughs, where he discovered new parks and neighborhoods, and attended more conferences. I spent countless hours searching for anything else that might be helpful to him, and eventually found a young adult life skills program for people with special needs. By this time, Craig had developed severe skepticism about any suggestions we or society promoted, so my best strategy was to show him an on-line site, then step back and hope. Fortunately, he followed through.. Unfortunately, at least initially, he had an experience that didn't work well for him:

A ... group that I went to in the city yesterday was a nightmare for me and conjured images from when I faced virtually the exact same thing in preschool, and now, years later, I can only react in the same clueless way. This is what happened in the group.

1) *Make a physical pose – any pose- and the person next in line says what he/she associates that pose with, and then comes up with their own pose and so forth. When I did my pose, which was meant to look like a drunkard or something, the next person just said I look like I'm way over thinking things (which made me feel rejected even though it wasn't the person's intent, because I was thinking hard and just don't know what is an interesting pose and even why I am doing it in the first place – is it to come up with something funny so others will laugh and then feel more comfortable around you?)*

2) *Then we went to a game like Zip-Zap-Zub which each says one of those words and then reaches out and points to another to say the next word in the sequence, and it gets faster each time and it usually ends up in laughter. For me, it makes me quite nervous that anyone can randomly point at me at any second, even if I didn't have to say anything or participate. There are other people with Asperger's in the group and*

while they were a bit slow and not sure how to do all of these things that happened in the group, they said they were benefitting and seemed to enjoy themselves a bit, which makes me feel more like an outsider and someone who is unable to be spontaneous in the way other people want.)

3) *The next thing was to pass around an ink-blot around the circle and say what we saw in it. I hate this with a passion, and I said it just looks like a child's bad scribbling. I was the only one who really didn't come up with some image.*

4) *Then we were told that the ink-blot was an image of a chair on a beach and we each individually are to go to the front of the room sitting in a chair and talk about what we imagine we're feeling at that beach. Some had difficulty with this, so a group leader waved her hand in front of people to get them in the fantasy land and then they said whatever. It actually made me annoyed because it assumed I had an ability that I didn't have, and for this and other events, I ended up saying I couldn't do it...*

5) *As I said, people in the group weren't quite good with imagining and often just said whatever they were thinking about their own lives, but the fact that they participated and said they benefitted while I became*

*more isolated didn't feel good. It got worse when
people "encouraged" me by saying, "just try it, we're all
accepting here and you don't have to worry. Come on.
Just try and experiment." Experiment doing what?
Tell me the experiment and how to do it and I'll do it!
This is where I definitely think that I'm not a human
and will never have a chance of identifying with most
people.*

The staff members didn't give up on him. Instead of
stepping away because he was so complicated, they
stepped forward. They didn't pigeon-hole Craig; rather,
they let him know he was valued. In particular, a young
woman (I'll call her Allie) who had just taken over as
Program Director genuinely cared about Craig, and
answered his hundreds of e-mails and phone calls over a
period of two years-and-a-half years. Craig felt like he had
a friend, and he did.

Thank you Allie, from a deep place in our hearts.

Chapter 16: Knowing

Written to his therapist in the day program:

I was just released from the hospital and was told I have an appointment with you on Thursday. However, this hospitalization has strongly discouraged me in terms of actually being able to get help from (the program) and the hospital when I need it the most. Here are my disorganized thoughts that I'm just putting out there. I know (the program) is overwhelmed with new people and poor staff to client ratios, and I really feel it in terms of the staff's availability to have time to talk with me even in crisis and I mean really talking in depth ...Also, when I was hospitalized this time, a ... psychiatrist used the analogy that if I could take a pill [going to the hospital] that would help me, even just very temporarily, I should take it. Well, guess what, I took the pill and now I have to deal with the effects of quickly going off the pill, which actually in many ways makes it worse than taking it in the first place! Combine that with (a caseworker in the hospital) telling me that I'm having fun over this whole thing of being hospitalized, I'm manipulative, and that I like being the center of attention and like taking up other people's time...I am very distrustful of getting help from anyplace I've tried thus far.

And in a separate e-mail:

So, I left a phone message with Lydia mentioning this but thought I should write it in an email too. My final decision, at least for the next several months and probably for the long-term, is to stop getting my treatment from (the program). It is NOT because I have any negative feelings towards Lydia or Dr. J. as in fact I mostly have good feelings and know you both care about me a lot. But I am frustrated/angry about the overload of people coming to (the program) and how it has lessened the ability of the staff to have sufficient time to work with me and especially in crises, and I'd rather have no support than just a little support and especially given that it's a place...that sensory-wise and depression-wise has been uncomfortable for me in the first place. Hopefully, that makes sense. I also hope to find some other avenue to get help --much luck is needed there! But in the meantime, I do need medications to be prescribed for me and I have about 3 weeks left...Thank you.

Craig Climbed a Tree

Craig's decision to stop getting his treatment was simultaneously positive and scary. He was gaining the maturity and independence to make a decision and move on. But he hadn't made arrangements to get a new psychiatrist and therapist who "got" him. When he found himself at the start of a downward spiral, he could afford to wait only a couple of days to process what was happening. And he was only willing to wait and process with the therapist and psychiatrist who had been working with him.

He couldn't tolerate explaining things more than once. He would say, "I've already said that." He was so complicated it took many meetings to begin to understand him. As a result, when Craig first began the day program, the team initially saw him as extremely manipulative. At the beginning of Craig's enrollment in the program, the team met with me, Ken, and Craig, and confronted us all with the manipulation that we allegedly permitted. Craig was furious; we were distressed and confused. Manipulation had always been a question we couldn't answer – was he, at times, arbitrarily and intentionally trying to wreak havoc on himself and those around him? Or was it something else? We didn't know what to believe, but it often seemed what we were doing wasn't working, so we constantly questioned ourselves.

Fran and Craig Wishnick

We questioned our parenting skills, methods and reactions, and were more than willing to make changes if we knew what to change and how. Maybe it was a healthy questioning, but it didn't feel good to be so conflicted about what we said and did. Their snap judgment was a new stress.

Over time, the day program team saw a bigger picture, and came to understand his complex and serious mental health difficulties. Craig heard words and concepts differently, and responded to how he heard information. The psychiatrist eventually apologized to us for his assumptions, for labeling much of Craig's behavior as manipulative. Manipulation was present, no doubt, but not as much as people initially assumed. And it was simplistic and unfair to make it the focus, given his real physical pain and many clear-cut disabilities.

Of great importance, during Craig's stay in the day program, his therapist made significant progress with him and helped him understand his anger towards us and others.

Until the point when Craig gained some insight, we had felt stymied no matter what we did. As a child, Craig believed that anything we said or did that was different (to him) from what we previously said or did, was a "lie." He held onto that well into his adult years. He believed we had lied to him many times. As a young adult, Craig was always urgently asking what he should do about situations he encountered. We didn't want to give him the answer, but rather tried to help him find it. But his stress was such that he couldn't seem to develop his options. He would demand an answer, reject it, demand a better answer. When we naturally pulled away or became frustrated, he believed we weren't helping him. It was a vicious cycle. His demands often felt like manipulation and resulted in turmoil.

One day we had a talk, and then received an e-mail from him that showed how he was re-processing some of his assumptions. While we didn't agree with all of it, his insights and re-calculations were helpful. They allowed us to begin better communication.

Dear Mother:

So my revelation I spoke of yesterday which helps me understand you is quite complicated for me to express but I'll try. First, sort of related, is that there are many times when things I've said have been interpreted as demands rather than requests, and that's because I somehow gave the impression that if the response I received isn't what I wanted, I couldn't accept it or would be upset...Now, here's my revelation: that on many occasions...you were telling me things you'd like me to do and then telling me I can/it's okay if I do something other than what you were requesting. But I felt suspicious and became frustrated because I felt my need for independence and figuring out what my own options are was not being met, and I actually still react that way when someone tells me what I can or cannot do, even if I know they're just trying to emphasize that it's a request. It helps me understand you a lot better, but I'm unsure of how to respond when this happens.

In a separate e-mail, he wrote:

*I'm realizing more about myself and how I usually seek people's approval not in words but in gestures, and the need for people to approve of me through their gestures is huge and cannot be overstated. If I don't receive the approval in gestures when I'm around others in a social environment, then I feel like a complete failure until I remove myself from that environment. Just one second of giving a light pleasant facial gesture to me when I say something that feels good, sounds thoughtful, or is positive for the other person goes a **very** long way, unless the gesture is exaggerated or strong in my mind, in which case I'd get scared.*

Given my sensitivity to gestures, you can imagine the degree of concern I have when I'm conscious that I'm giving negative gestures, even if I'm aware that people are not reacting strongly to the gestures (I look for the slightest indication that it's related to me by comparing the way people react facially to other people as compared to me so it's not based on my worry, although my worry heightens how closely I'm analyzing things.) When I'm having a day when I'm giving negative gestures, which can be due to feeling tired, panicky, nervous, cynical, hopeless, depressed, etc. I almost feel obligated to stay away from people because the interactions are likely to leave me feeling bad about myself and responsible for bringing others down, even if bringing others down was just for a split second and then they enjoyed my company and moved past the gestures. If you have any ideas on this, let me know because my sensitivity has led to dramatic personal improvements, but also leaves me quite vulnerable, even to unintended gestures with positive intentions.

Having left the day program, Craig scrambled to find a new therapist and psychiatrist, with help from us and the program. He ended up finding both, but there was a significant problem with lack of communication with the new medical team even though they had received his medical records and talked with the therapist from the day program. The new psychiatrist wouldn't look at Craig while she spoke. She sat at a desk facing the wall, focusing on the computer screen in front of her while Craig sat behind her. For a subsequent appointment, Craig asked Ken to accompany him, and Ken saw the problems first-hand. As they began, Craig could see the computer and observed the psychiatrist looking at someone else's record. After that was "corrected," Ken observed what Craig had described: the only time the psychiatrist even glanced at Craig was when she needed to fill out a question about his facial expression. It was distressing that she considered this professional and effective.

I'll pause here from Craig's narrative to say something about electronic records and their creation, and enabling quick and easy access to medical information. Medical providers must remember: this is a tool that should be used with great care. Face-to-face contact with the client—a human being in distress—is imperative, for many reasons. Mental health clients often feel isolated and misunderstood. Having their team member watch a computer screen rather than the client only accentuates the disconnectedness. In addition, while it should go without saying, I'll say it anyway: having the wrong file or client computer screen is completely inexcusable. Know who you are meeting with.

We called and requested transfer to another psychiatrist. Craig asked me to go with him to the second appointment with this new psychiatrist because he felt that the magnitude of his depression, anxiety and daily difficulties wasn't being understood. The new psychiatrist told Craig that there was no such medication as liquid Ativan for his anxiety. This was a medicine that had worked well for Craig in the day program. I took off from work and accompanied Craig to the appointment, and we met with both the therapist and psychiatrist. In front of me, they scolded Craig, saying, "Why did you need to bring your mother? You could have described what was happening yourself. Your goal is to be more independent."

I worked to control my fury in front of Craig, but proceeded to tell them that indeed Craig had previously and successfully been prescribed liquid Ativan and that it was in his record. I also described what Craig's prior weeks had been like, in more detail than Craig could describe. The team eventually stopped their scolding and listened, but it wasn't the last time, in several settings, that Craig experienced mental health professionals using their clients' independence goals against them.

Fortunately, over time, Craig and his new therapist began to build trust and work together well. Craig was frequently e-mailing and occasionally meeting with Allie, at the Manhattan program. He continued to experience depression, anxiety, frustration and confusion, but he also developed a stronger desire to be engaged with the world. In the midst of all his ongoing issues, he was about to take many steps forward.

Chapter 17: Changing

In 2010, Craig turned twenty-six. He wanted to be independent, to expand his interests, and he tried to make sense of his place in the world. Too often he felt too sick to get out of bed and still didn't have a job or real friends. He struggled and tried; he was by turns fragile and troubled, determined and resourceful. We saw his different sides appear to fight each other – the enormous strengths battling the serious illnesses and deficits. We witnessed his struggles and were often drawn into them.

A series of 2010 e-mails from Craig portrays his emotional state. Many were written to us while he was a few feet away in our home. Others came from him in his rented room in town, a few miles from our home.

1/01/10

Subject: fingers being much colder than hands – tendonitis

When we see Dr. Syed, a priority that may even be higher than heartburn is the tendonitis I have that is making my fingers cold and sore, and the fingers connecting to pain I have in my wrist. If I don't wear my wrist things regularly, there's a bit of pain.

1/01/10

Subject: fascinating video on Seattle transit

I just watched a fascinating video on Seattle transit and read a couple of blogs. I've decided that now would NOT be the time to go to Seattle, so if I were going to the West Coast, I'd visit Portland for a day or 2 (it's really a vastly white population with not as much racial diversity as I'd look for but it would be interesting to walk around the green areas) and Vancouver for a few days. I'm also thinking about whether I should go to Chicago for the Star Trek Convention ...

1/03/10

Subject: place I was mentioning

http://www.selaverde.com/lang/en/ is the place I was mentioning. It might be difficult to coordinate ...but the pictures are so great.

1/05/10

Subject: problem with meds

I haven't taken my morning meds 2 of the past 3 mornings even though I thought I did this morning.

Craig Climbed a Tree

1/05/10

Subject: actually, never mind about meds

I was wrong about being wrong, I did take my morning meds today...

1/05/10

Subject: While looking at Santa Cruz, Bolivia

While looking for possible trips to Santa Cruz, Bolivia ($10 hostel and an exciting place, which I think would be near my top in terms of priority in Latin America), I started reading the rules of social etiquette...I really like the way this is worded and think we can all learn from this, especially here in the US. "If you are sitting between or beside people, **never turn your back on someone in order to pay attention to what another is saying.** *It is considered very bad social etiquette, even a snub if you will to "dar la espalda "(turn your back on someone). If it is absolutely necessary for some reason...you should say "Disculpe si le doy la espalda un momento" ("forgive me for turning my back on you for a moment.") This will let them know you are aware of them, are not snubbing them, and have no intention of being rude."*

1/06/10

Subject: really scared around people

I pushed myself to go to Starbucks and sit there, but for the past couple of days, I'm really afraid of people, and when I hear (his landlady) my knees are shaking and everything...

1/09/10

Subject: Decided I definitely want to go

I've decided I'm sold on going to Costa Rica and spending at least a couple of nights in a family-owned hostel I like the sound of in Monteverde and exploring tons of nearby preserves etc. And then probably going to Tamarindo, Samara, or another beach area with a hostel I can stay in. I definitely won't be going to the Selva Verde because of the price.

1/09/10

Subject: reconsidering trip

I'm reconsidering the trip. Although I'd still like to stay in the same hostel I mentioned, I've watched some YouTube videos and while the Monteverde preserves look beautiful, I think that I'd want the focus of any trip to be learning new things. I really want to be in the rainforest and eat fresh pineapple, and meet indigenous people (or close to indigenous) in Guatil, Costa Rica. Or take a hike lasting a couple of days where I can meet new people.

His e-mail to Amazon:

Hello – This is not a question about an order I placed but rather on product reviews I have written. Many years back, when I was using my parent's e-mail account, I wrote reviews for products for some cds I purchased. However, I was not aware at the time that by writing reviews, that anytime someone searched on Google for my parent's names, my reviews would show up. Can you advise me on if there is anything me or my parents can do to delete the reviews, as it is not the kind of profile they would like to have on the internet? Thanks.

1/21/10

Subject: borderline on needing hospitalization

I'm borderline right now on if I need to be hospitalized...my depression and anxiety is high and I'm unable to get myself to go to the internship...

1/21/10

Subject: Feeling okay enough

It turns out that I needed 14 hours of sleep rather than 12 ½ hours to feel okay enough to at least say I can stay out of the hospital. I'm struggling hard to be in control of this...

1//27/10

Subject: reason of heartburn

I just came up with a pretty good idea of why I've recently had heartburn and it makes sense. After Scruffy helped me, I felt a sudden bit of heartburn, which helped me theorize that it could be a way of getting stuff through my system that's normally having hard time going through...

1/30/10

Subject: just a reminder-during conversations.

Just a reminder that during conversations, it's <u>really really</u> important that you don't say at the end of a sentence "you know" in a suddenly cheerful way. What happens is then I try to respond to everything before the "you know" so I don't end of hearing that part, but then I end up not listening or communicating well.

1/30/10

Hi-So we just talked over the phone and you let me know that you're skittish and everything because of my mood that I've had most of the day. Please remember that a week or so ago...I was worried about how I'd make it through this given how the medical condition and not eating much add to my depression I already have. You tried to be supportive and said we'd make it through this and you'd do everything you could to help out. I really appreciate the intention. At the same time, it seems you overestimate how much you can help out...Just some thoughts in the few minutes today that I'm thinking clearly.

2/04/10

Subject: Can we make this – avocado brulee

This recipe looks amazing but don't know if we have/need a blowtorch or other equipment mentioned to make this avocado brulee.

2/07/10

Subject: lack creative ability for conversations

I really lack the creative ability to have conversations different than what I've naturally done – I really hope the psychiatrist is willing to change around my meds on Tuesday.

2/08/10

Subject: helpful idea

I just heard a helpful idea listening to an interview with a songwriter who I like: "what decision would I make if I loved the world rather than trying to fix the world." It's a very feminine feeling (i.e. you can't love and try to fix something at the same time), but there is a good point in that message.

2/15/10

Subject: understand why mom likes HGTV at night

After dealing with E-Bay for a little over an hour today, I think I understand why mom likes HGTV so much at night. Even though it's a bit artificially cheerful and not looking much at the complexities, it's one of the few channels on TV that's intended to be calming and positive relation and energy oriented. Maybe that's also a good part of the reason women like low key conversations that's not really about anything – as an alternative to things unlike their general style that they've dealt with during the day. Hmm...

2/23/10

Subject: It's as bad as a redneck, comes out as fast as Theo's (our other dog) licks

It's as bad as a redneck and comes as fast as Theo's (our other dog) licks. Any guess what I'm referring to...? My gassing ever since leaving All Sport today, and which I'll need to tell the G.I. doctor about.

3/09/10

Subject: much relief

I decided based on what you said to just put eye drops in my eye and directly at the sore areas. I did and feel much relief. I think I'll be able to actually relax this evening, which will be nice!

3/18/10

Subject: the tick and advice

So I scheduled an appointment at Family Practice. They're likely to prescribe me antibiotics, which I've never been able to have effectively because it worsens my depression, but a nursing assistant here thinks I'll likely need it because the tick is deeply embedded...And what do you think I should do?

4/09/10

Subject: Being praised and culture (sent to a coworker in his volunteer "internship" with copy sent to us.

So, I tend to be culturally a bit different than people here when they receive praise from others. I'm a lot more like the Japanese, and when they are praised, the emphasis is on making themselves appear to be equal to and no better than others, even though they may internally accept the praise. I know that especially among Hispanic men, it's almost the opposite and being praised a lot means having higher status etc. Just so you know! And I do appreciate that others notice what I'm doing and connecting.

4/10/10

Subject: what they thought of me

I'm curious what Chris and Anna (people he didn't know) thought of me today. I was trying to be happy and friendly at the same time that I'm pretty out of it and just wanting to relax...which is why I decided it would be better to come home after the walk. I enjoyed their company but didn't get to talk to Chris as much as I wanted.

4/13/10

Subject: found where I'd live in DC

*I found where I'd live in DC if I could afford it –
almost without a doubt – Woodley Park/Adams Morgan,
near the zoo.*

4/23/10

Subject: May I know of your May trip?

May I know the date of your May trip to the farm? =)

4/23/10

Subject: May I know of your May trip?

*Well tomorrow I'm foraging in the city. I was
thinking of cancelling it because I don't want to wake up
early to take the train etc. but I keep rescheduling and so I
should probably just go since tomorrow will be a very nice
day for foraging. So it'll have to be Sunday.*

4/29/10

Subject: One more thing I should mention

*One thing I can do is not bring valuables to the
James Taylor/Carole King concert and keep things in a
locker in a hostel in Harlem, so when I go I wouldn't be too
worried about something being stolen*

5/31/10

Subject: Really good site – your opinion?

*So this is a site related to a NYC Borderline
Personality Disorder meet up group I attend. I'd like your
reaction because it's so honest and represents what the
group is like – and the doctor speaking will be a guest on*

the 7th – I'd have to decide whether to attend that or the bipolar group.

6/05/10

Subject: Bowery Club FAQ's

I was thinking of attending a $8 performance at the Bowery Poetry Club in July for the 10th annual Woody Guthrie Birthday Bash. I was looking at the Bowery FAQ's and they're funny!

6/24/10

To: Allie (with copy sent to Mother)

...Here are some really personal issues I'd like to discuss when we meet tomorrow at 2 – can't believe all that there is to discuss – can the brain be more complicated?

... This is going to be <u>REALLY</u> deep – hope it's okay with you because I need help processing some more): As I forwarded in a previous email, I now believe after hearing an expert on BPD speak in the city that I have Borderline Personality Disorder along with Asperger's as the primary diagnosis. I, as well as my family and probably my psychiatrist after talking with him, believe I have BPD because I feel the need to "test" relationships because I have a hard time believing people care about me even if there are all the signs that they do care. I usually test relationships when I haven't heard from the person in a *while ...I've chased people away with, in my opinion, a pretty rude and unjustified response that I still feel I need to do anyway (want to change this if you can help me). I especially test relationships when I've recently received inconsistent responses from people, but then my response to what I see as inconsistent starts to create intense emotional and back and forth relationships...However, needing tense emotional relationships seems at odds with the emotional detachment, for lack of better words, that the Asperger's label would indicate I have...*

This would be a great discussion if we have even more time. An analogy of the discrepancy between the way Bob Dylan comes across (snotty) vs. actual intelligence in writing, and perhaps I am similar, even though I think I respect and care more about others at the same time I may come across similar to Dylan.

It was July, 2010. Craig announced he had given notice to Elaine, would be vacating his room, and was moving to New York City. A flood of thoughts and feelings enveloped us: Craig was giving up his room without even having a place in the city! We knew how hard it is to find a decent place to live in—how could he do it, find a place on his limited SSI allotment?

On the other hand, moving away was an age-appropriate act of maturity. We knew Craig liked the city's anonymity and opportunities for engagement. He would need to connect immediately with decent mental health providers there, and transfer his SSI, Medicaid and Food Stamps. Should we allow him to go? What would it mean for us when he inevitably called us, in crisis?

We thought, we discussed, we dared to hope. Maybe Craig could find more of a sense of purpose in the city. A meaningful job, a friend, maybe. A *life*.

Fran and Craig Wishnick

Chapter 18: Walking Home

Subject: list of great things I've attended in NYC
(from my memory)
7/23/10
Silvio Rodriguez Concert
James Taylor and Carole King Concert
Pat Humphries and Holly Near Concert at People's
Voice Café
Phil Ochs Song Night Concert at People's Voice Café
Inti-Illimani Concert at Americas Society
Howie Mandell at 92nd Street Y
Isabel Allende at 92nd Street Y
BPD (Borderline Personality Disorder) Group
Cloisters Museum and Wave Hill Trips
MAS Architectural Tours of GCT, Boerum Hill and
Wall St.
French and American Architecture Day Lectures at
Center for Architecture in the Village

Jack Eichenbaum's tour – How the 7 Line Changed Queens

Colbert Report (2 times, including guest Paul Simon!)

Daily Show with guest Brian Williams

Who Wants to be a Millionaire TV show

People's Court TV Show

Regis and Kelly TV Show

Martha Stewart TV Show

Center stage TV Show with guest Bill O'Reilly

China and India Day Lectures – Institute for Public Knowledge

Mexican Youth and Families Day Lectures

Governors Island with Bike N Roll

Columbia University Series Day Lectures with Amy Goodman

Greenwich Village Foods of New York Tour

Art Tour in Brooklyn – Immigrant Heritage

2 Yankees Games

Human Rights by Region Day Lectures at Columbia University

Craig wrote that list almost exactly a year before his death on July 27, 2011. What happened between making that list and his final days is a story in itself.

Fran and Craig Wishnick

In late July, 2010, Craig decided to move to New York City. Realizing it was a move toward independence, more opportunities for activities, therapy, possible friendships, and volunteer opportunities or employment, my husband and I gulped, worked through our fears, and supported his decision. Through the online site Craig's List, ironically, Craig found a room in an apartment in Washington Heights, interviewed with the housemates, and they chose him. It's important to say they chose him, because Craig could be intriguing, personable, and funny for short periods of time. His difficulties with connecting often emerged later on, in day-to-day interactions, from misunderstandings and missed social cues. When he realized people were frowning or laughing at him, or annoyed, his anxiety went through the roof. Combined with his naturally high anxiety and bouts of depression, the result was isolation. Plus, Craig never had longstanding friendships, not as a child, not as a young adult. He never had the experience of give and take, all that goes into establishing and maintaining relationships. He didn't know how to keep connections going, and had many questions about rules of engagement. He was still experiencing debilitating flare-ups of ulcerative colitis, too.

It is amazing that Craig persevered. But he did.

Craig Climbed a Tree

Upon moving to the Washington Heights apartment, Craig had difficulties from the beginning, with housemates and with the systems he needed for support. He also had difficulties with himself.

Little things built up. For example, he filled up their fridge with produce and other items, because he didn't have much experience cooking, didn't have the money to go out to eat, and was used to seeing lots of food at our house. His housemates told him his food was taking too much space. Since he took things literally, he wanted them to show him exactly how much space was his. He didn't get a clear answer, so Craig began to keep items in his room.

So the produce was being preserved better than I thought but I started disliking the strong smell of that in my room (even with the produce preserving bags and a closed container) combined with the fact that I killed a loud hissing cockroach during the night! So I put the produce saving bags in the fridge with the salads ...I was just trying to come up with options given that they seemed so limited and I needed to stop hearing about the fridge. Anyway, I just looked around the Bronx today and walked around a few grocery stores that I think I'd like working in and I found a couple of places with great produce prices, so

I think I could go there and just shop more frequently as my housemates are suggesting.

He had to transfer his food stamps, Medicaid, and Social Security Disability (SSI) to the city. He wanted to do this by himself or at least to find assistance by himself. The Social Security transfer worked out fine. The others, not so much, and with every problem he couldn't fix, Craig lost confidence.

Things are a nightmare for me at Food Stamps. I went to the office for a 4th time today, waiting 4 hours, and then was told that ...I need a Con Edison bill (and they wouldn't allow me to talk with or put someone else on the phone to help me understand all this because they say it's against their policy!!!) However, the Con Edison bill isn't addressed to me but to the person here collecting rent, and he threw away the bill after he paid it last month. So now I'm in the position where I have no food stamps (they made me wait until food stamps from my previous county ended) and I might not have it for the entire month. Plus, the person I spoke to was actually rude.

He called us repeatedly and asked for advice, but wished he could do it himself. Frankly, the systems of transfer from one county to another aren't clear-cut or user-friendly, and we learned how especially true that was in NYC. As Craig said to us once, wistfully, "I guess they don't expect people like me to move." Craig tried to work with advocacy agencies in the city, but he didn't get the assistance that he wanted and needed. Finally, Craig asked me to take time off from work and come into the city. Even as an experienced system navigator, I had a distressing experience. Eventually we worked it out, but the resolution included Craig's unfortunate realization that he couldn't have done it himself. It didn't help his feelings of anxiety, fear, and limited self-worth.

Recognizing how Craig was continuing to have a difficult and isolating time, Ken went into the city on several occasions and met up with Craig to explore neighborhoods, try restaurants, and just talk. Those days were good ones. Ken wishes he had done it more. Much more.

Craig had problems at the mental health provider he had carefully selected, at a renowned NYC hospital. Craig navigated public transit and the city streets, but had to sit and wait, with some delays in excess of thirty minutes, without explanation or apology. For a person with anxiety, the not-knowing was intolerable. Craig had worked hard to master the art of advocating for himself. But after he went up to the receptionist and complained about the delays, his psychiatrist reprimanded him, saying that he thought that Craig was trying to fire him.

Fran and Craig Wishnick

Next he encountered problems with what is called the "Medicaid Utilization Threshold Program," which specifies the number of units of pharmacy services that a client is eligible for in a benefit year. Since Craig's doses of medications for depression and anxiety and ulcerative colitis frequently changed and he had problems with poison ivy and skin irritations, he went back to his doctors often to request an override of the threshold. Otherwise, he couldn't continue to fill his prescriptions. His anxiety increased each time that happened, especially when doctors didn't take care of the override application in a timely manner.

Craig's housemates were yelling at him about cooking in the morning, and noise. It's hard to have housemates, but for Craig, without a job, without friends, with all his issues, it was overwhelming. Yet he tried to figure it out:

> *My housemate is being a pain in the butt and says when he hears the curtain fall (needs to be repaired) and me lightly moving stuff around during normal hours that he knows I'm banging things against the wall. I wish he'd just come out and say that he's sensitive to sounds because he really is, but instead he just talks about the thin walls, respecting and living with others etc. rather than accepting personal responsibility like I did. When I hear too many*

issues told to me at once, I get overwhelmed...Do you have
suggestions with how to be sensitive while giving people
feedback that they're asking for/expecting too much...?

Within a few months, Craig realized he needed to find different housing. The final straw for him was when he got bedbugs. One night, he called us after rashes popped out. Ironically, he had seen his new primary care physician in the city for the first time that morning, before the rashes had emerged. Not recognizing the bedbug phenomenon, he thought he had poison ivy again, but we guessed it was probably bedbugs, and suggested he call his doctor in the morning, and take a bus to our house afterwards, to spend a few days relaxing.

What happened next is almost indescribable. That morning, he had a therapist appointment. His anxiety had been climbing because of all that was happening to him in the city, as well as natural fluctuations in his mood. When he arrived for his therapy appointment, his therapist saw his highly anxious and depressed state, and heard his complaints about rashes (which could have been caused by his medication). She walked him to the hospital's emergency room and spoke to someone behind the scenes. Meanwhile, Craig left a message to let us know he didn't think he would be coming to our house, because his therapist was arranging for him to get care, and he'd see us another time. I still have that poignant recorded message on my cell phone.

The hospital staff took Craig's cell phone and wallet and put him in a psychiatric emergency holding room for evaluation. He wasn't seen by a psychiatrist for over 8 hours. During that time, he wasn't able to get any of his medication and was in a room with several screaming mental health clients.

We had no idea this was happening until an emergency room psychiatrist called us in the middle of the night. By that time, Craig had lost it, and the psychiatrist reported that he was crying heavily. Wouldn't you be? She asked about his history and, in light of his suicidal ideations, decided to admit him. I asked how we could get more information about his condition or speak with him, and was told I could talk to the attending psychiatrist in the morning.

We didn't sleep. When I called the next morning, Craig had calmed down, and the attending psychiatrist didn't feel he needed to be an inpatient. He confirmed that the rashes were from bedbugs and told me what we needed to do to get rid of them. I took a very deep breath and made a request. Since Craig had been through so much, could they hold him for a few hours while my husband drove to the city to pick him up from the hospital? We thought Craig needed and deserved some special care, and we needed to see him. The psychiatrist said yes. Ninety minutes later, with my husband on his way to the city, Craig called. They had discharged him, and he was walking back to his room alone.

Chapter 19: Questions and Contradictions

In early 2011, Craig moved out of his Washington
Heights room. He couldn't tolerate several of his
housemates, and they couldn't tolerate him. His
experiences receiving mental health services in the
neighborhood were untenable, and he hoped to switch
them upon moving into new housing. It was painful for us
to watch and attempt to comfort him, as an overload of
considerations made his days and decisions highly
stressful. He knew switching neighborhoods would likely
mean a new Medicaid managed care plan, as well as
notifying Social Security and food stamps, so he was
trying to be careful in making the change.

Craig counted on a room in Queens as his next step,
but got tricked into giving a cash deposit for what turned
out to be a scam. Angst about the loss of that deposit
money ate away at him. He always had a hard time with
money issues – he went over and over his meager $761

SSI allotment, trying to figure out how to manage. He had believed the man who deceived him. He thought he seemed nice. Craig even thought they could be friends. He couldn't accept that this guy whose facial expression and gestures indicated kindness could have scammed him. It didn't matter that a neighborhood police detective told Craig the scammer had done this many times. Craig had worked hard most of his life to learn facial expressions, and naively wanted to believe that he could figure out people from their face, movements, and what he called their "energy."

He tried every angle he and we could think of to find housing, including a match-up service for senior citizens who wanted a roommate, any age, to help pay expenses. But Craig's tight budget, in a city with little affordable housing, and his other requirements, like easy accessibility to mass transit and non-smoking housemates, severely limited his options. On his e-mail, I found one of the many messages he had posted:

Does anyone know of a quiet, laid back living situation that's available, or maybe someone else reading this post is looking for places too and we can search together? ...What I'm looking for is mainly a quiet (non-party), non-smoking, relaxed environment and ideally I'd be living with people who love animals (wouldn't be *bringing pets of my own) and are into healthy living since I'm a vegetarian and Park Slope Co-op member, or with people who just like to talk casually during their spare time...we don't need to be best friends or anything – just easygoing and good communication. I'm pretty quiet and will be spending a lot of my time doing dog walking for a non-profit and attending NYU, Columbia University and New School events. If living with a Senior, I'm open to grocery shopping for you, walking your dogs or doing extra chores in the house in exchange for the lower rent, as $600 with all utilities included is the max I can pay for now. Westchester County (near Metro North Line), Inwood in Manhattan, Forest Hills and Rego Park in Queens, and Crown Heights and Park Slope in Brooklyn are my favorite neighborhoods, but I'm open to others if it's the right match. Hope to hear back from you soon!*

It's ironic to think about Craig wanting, "easygoing and good communication." While he desperately wanted it, easygoing, casual communication with Craig was an oxymoron. Conversations with him were mostly intense. All his life, Craig had problems telling and listening to stories. Since everything was black-and-white, literal, when a person told Craig a story he needed it to be completely clear in his mind. He wrote:

February 2011

Craig Climbed a Tree

...When someone is telling me a story about something going on in their life, I try to relate by asking a couple of questions, but usually each question I have isn't answered clearly in a way that I feel is addressing the heart of the question so each question usually ends up leading to many more questions. For the other person, if they're trying to tell me a story and I keep asking questions back to back, they can often feel put on the spot, defensive, and generally uncomfortable. Further, my questions become very un-casual as I have to ask more because I'm frustrated that I'm having to ask in so many ways to get to the point where I understand well enough that I can relate (unless they simplify their story.) Since others need less questions asked and for it to be casual in order to feel they're relating to me, I'm wondering if you have any ideas or suggestions?

After searching far and wide on many lists, he found a short-term room rental in an Irish neighborhood in the city. But wherever he was, Craig was Craig, and while trying to deal with his depression, anxiety, and ulcerative colitis flare-ups, with job and his social difficulties, he held tightly to a belief that he could do better with people if he understood the behavior of those around him to guide him. He wrote:

February 2011

I've made a few cultural mistakes living here in an Irish neighborhood...I have a tough road ahead with Freud's quote "This is one race of people for whom psychoanalysis is of no use whatsoever...I'm reading up on Irish behavior ....

Craig was always trying to figure out how to relate:

March 2011

I have a question about being conversational with people and figuring out how to relate, particularly when I'm not feeling well. With "normal" or neuro-typical people, if they're not feeling well very once in a while and have a challenging day that affects their own stability, it might work well for them to reach out to a friend to talk casually, .and then ask the friend for support. However, for people like me with depression and who are regularly working on maintaining our own stability...it's hard...it's very difficult to censor ourselves when we're not feeling well... ...I guess a key question here is how do you become a good listener and become interested even if you're not feeling interested and this is a fairly constant occurrence? Of course, there are times I have fun and it's not that difficult...

I try to say things tactfully, but then the strategy messes up later when I'm wearing down and my ability to filter isn't there as well, which can also be a problem when my physical space suddenly becomes limited or hypersensitivity to something huge causes me to panic.

Craig tried to deal with his perceptions of communication inconsistencies. Over the years, when expressing his needs in an increasingly forceful and distressed manner, he was told he was manipulative or power-grabbing. We sometimes told him the same. Yet he felt that he could only function by getting what he needed—clear and literal answers—answers we and others couldn't always give. It seemed to Craig that the whole world was full of contradictions, especially about what was expected of him.

He asked the leader of a group he had joined to include this issue:

March 2011

I think a really good possible group discussion topic would be when asking for what we need through assertiveness becomes/is seen as demanding or even a power attempt. I learned in DBT and other courses that as long as we clearly communicate what we want/need/feel and leave space for the other person to react and actively listen to their reaction, we've behaved assertively and if the other person has a bad negative reaction, that's their "problem" – beyond our control – because we've done our part. Indeed, we are often encouraged in our society to say what's on our minds...So how do we tell how much to ask for --not be "too needy" even if it's asked in an assertive manner, even when it's spread out over time, at what point will it likely be overwhelming for others, and how do we react when others may see it as demanding...

I don't think Craig ever got answers to these almost impossible questions.

Chapter 20: New Year's Wishes

Despite all of his challenges, our son had a quirky sense of humor, and could be funny in an offbeat way when observing and mimicking human behavior.

Subject: Happy New Year (with plenty of adjectives)

...I hope you have an accomplished, achieving, awesome, beautiful, balanced, bright, emancipated, empowered, energized, exuberant, fantastic, fulfilled, gratifying, harmonious, joyful, peaceful, positive, prosperous, radiant, serene, triumphant, warm, wonderful and happy new year! I figured people like using adjectives in their wishes for others right now so I'd join in!=}

Nonetheless, he saw himself as different, confused and cynical. In a way that was sometimes distressing to me, Craig was judgmental if people weren't straightforward, philosophical or seemed "too happy." With others, when he revealed his depression and anxiety or tried to join in, people inevitably pulled away. Craig penned:

Fran and Craig Wishnick

This quote below from a Star Trek episode is exactly what I'm feeling – and much of it really well expressed.

"They tolerate you Odo because you emulate them...But even when you [Odo] make yourself in their image, they know you are not truly one of them. They know that what you appear to be does not reflect who you really are. It's only a mask. What lies underneath is alien to them, and so they fear it, and that fear can turn to hate in the blink of an eye."

I know this quote borders on being too cynical and generalizing about people, but it definitely reflects the very heart of a feeling I've been having for a long time. Making myself in their image means focusing on using playful voices and trying to be sensitive to how others get afraid when I express emotional vulnerability...but it may be that I'm just different.

Nowadays, on-line searches reveal that it isn't unusual for people with Asperger's to have connections with the themes and characters on Star Trek. Our son was fascinated by the Star Trek series and in particular two characters: Data and Seven-of-Nine. In one episode, Seven-of-Nine laments how she didn't "... understand the rules for this type of social occasion." She was advised to choose a group of people and "chime in," to join the discussion. She did, with disastrous results. Craig's other favorite character, the android called Data, was clueless as he tried to analyze and understand human behavior. In the series, Data was eventually given an "emotional chip" to deliver appropriate emotions, but still found it hard to master them.

Craig identified with Data.

Ken and I remember many times when Craig asked us to watch certain episodes of Star Trek with him, and talk about it afterwards. I think he wanted us to feel his pain. We did, more than he ever knew. We ourselves were and are not comfortable in many social situations, either. We've often asked ourselves how people learn the intricacies of human interaction and have concluded the obvious: through a lifetime of observation and practice. Without childhood and young adult friendships, Craig didn't have much practice. Most of us experience confusion about what to do in our relationships. Craig only felt comfortable when he had literal answers.

April 2011

Subject: Social dancing...taking "no, it's not necessary" at face value and insisting on things? Bcc: mother

I'm struggling to figure out when people offer me things (i.e. a meal out) or when I've offered something to someone and get the response, "no, it's not necessary", how much social dancing I really need to do with the back and forth/insisting on something which is so typical of many social interactions I've seen...I really want to know more about the bare minimum I need to do of this social dancing! ...

During the spring of 2011, he came to this conclusion about relationships and stress:

Anyway, my realization is that since people are quite stressed out in their own lives and have enough serious things to be concerned/worried about, they are always looking to befriend people who they perceive are at a lower stress level than them. If they perceive this other person to be at a higher stress level...that does not necessarily stop a friendship from being formed, but is a major setback...So the key is to make people perceive you're not as stressed out as you are...until they form a friendship which makes each other comfortable and confident...then it is more acceptable to show vulnerabilities etc. because they already understand each other well enough that they can't hide or fake things as easily...

Yet, even with all his issues, Craig made the most of his time in New York City. He would depart the subway at random stops and explore neighborhoods in a way that I suspect most New Yorkers wouldn't have the courage to do. He found hidden parks and community events that excited him, such as "Community Dialogue Among Caribbean/Latin American Immigrants in New York City," and "A Forgotten Conflict...The Role of External Actors in the Northern Uganda Conflict." He also found free entertainment:

> *Subject: Finally stumbled on this (have been looking for this forever in so many ways)*
>
> *Finally stumbled upon this – have been looking for Broadway singers performing at Times Square and Central Park and had trouble finding it for this year, but these are at Bryant Park*

Due to his limited budget, Craig explored the city with his own food and drink, but occasionally allowed himself a take-out vegetarian meal, and called us immediately afterwards about his finds. "You just have to try this," he would say. When we picked up the phone, we never knew what question, emergency, or delight would be in store for us.

Sometimes, I admit, we just didn't answer the phone. We had to allow ourselves to breathe.

Despite Craig's love of New York City, he couldn't continue to live there. he couldn't afford to live on his own, and couldn't find a roommate situation that worked for him. He knew he needed to get proper mental health treatment, but couldn't until he found a stable place to live. His location would dictate his insurance, and his insurance would dictate the treatment providers that he could access.

When he was able, with great resourcefulness and determination, Craig explored Westchester County options. Neighborhoods, clinics and providers, places to walk and hike, where to take public transit and shop—and, maybe, work. He poured over rental possibilities and found one with a Chinese owner. With his quirky sense of humor, he wrote:

4/10/11

Subject: really wish I could consider this in Hartsdale right now

He printed a Craig's list rental and wrote: do you know how I can learn Chinese in one day?

His complicated housing needs—low rent, safe location accessible to public transit, non-smoking, quiet, a landlord willing to accept someone unemployed—made his housing search difficult, if not impossible. So he asked us to move to Westchester. We declined. He pursued us relentlessly, prodding us to buy him a place. Craig being Craig, he wouldn't let go. He wanted to know if there was any price that we could afford, just so he could have a hole in the wall he could call his own. In long family talks, he repeatedly told us that having a place he could count on would give him some desperately needed certainty and stability. We dared to just say no. Was this tough love? Was it past time to think about ourselves, and stop "saving" him? Privately, and with intensity, Ken and I talked about whether we should leave him to it, to somehow figure things out. But Craig's desperation was palpable, and he was trying to make a life despite his obstacles.

We were at our wits end. We knew that we weren't going to move, and fervently hoped that something good would kick in for him.

Chapter 21: Churning

While Craig was searching for another place to live, he worked hard to find free activities that kept him engaged, when he could get out of bed:

Subject: Interesting meetup I'll be attending this Friday – Trash Tour

...Join us to explore the areas' wasted food and other goods and to gather food for our feast on Saturday. We give advice on how to salvage these goods and comment on the reasons for such waste...Do you want to reduce your consumer impact on the earth, humans and animals?...

Then, suddenly, hope seemed to emerge. He found a place: a co-op apartment in Westchester that was actually inexpensive enough for us to consider buying it for him. We were skeptical, unsure of what we wanted to do, but went with Craig to see it. We were prepared for a dump; instead, it turned out to need minor repairs. We could imagine Craig living there. Despite misgivings, but in an effort to keep trying for Craig, we eventually got an accepted offer for $45,000. Craig wanted to be there and began visualizing how he would set things up. I still have the color slip that he chose for the bathroom.

We hit a brick wall. After sending the co-op board masses of paperwork, proving we would make the purchase and Craig would pay the monthly maintenance fee, the co-op board met—violating their own rules requiring the applicant to be present—and turned Craig down. At first we believed there had to be some recourse. However, after talking with an attorney, and a non-profit that works with folks with disabilities, we realized that the law does not require the co-op board to explain their actions. In fact, co-ops routinely turn people down, and we were unlikely to win a legal battle. Still, we tried to be upbeat for Craig. We encouraged Craig to write a note to a housing advocate. He wrote:

> *5/4/11*
>
> *Subject: Details about co-op and questions*
>
> *Thanks very much for your call and your concern about my challenging situation right now! As mentioned over the phone, I'm attaching the information. In the meantime, I have a few questions for you: I would very much like to find a way of living in the Hartsdale/White Plains/Westchester area for the long-term. As we talk and*

you get to know me, I'm wondering if you can keep me in mind when you talk to other people to see if someone else you know might need some help with chores, errands, pet walking, etc. in exchange for reduced rent up to $600. It's pretty isolating to feel rejected and discriminated against like this, and I really want to be somehow proactive

After much discussion, he had to back down and return to our town. Right at that time, his name was called for a subsidized unit close to our home. He wrote:

Here is a very realistic budget for what it would like while I'm living in housing near you.

$325	*utilities*
$160	*acupuncture*
$161	*Trailways – unless you can pay for that*
$ 60	*food in NYC*
$ 40	*hotel night(s) in city*
$ 28	*gym and transit to gym and mental health*
$ 30	*groceries or coffee/cheese from city stores*
$ 25	*transit in NYC*
$ 20	*events in NYC*
$ 15	*house organization and clothing items*
$ 10	*PAWS (a dog rescue organization)*

donation

$ 5	*laundry not done at parents*

Craig Climbed a Tree

Donation to an animal charity, acupuncture, gyms, New York city trips? Those were the life-affirming things that made Craig feel like a person, which made him imagine possibilities for himself, and gave him some pleasure. He was ill, felt distraught, worthless, and often suicidal—yet he kept trying to figure out how to survive. Tried to understand his world.

We continued to allow him to make decisions for himself. We watched, with stomachs churning.

Chapter 22: Enough

For years, Craig was on doses of benzodiazepines (benzos) and other medications. Doctors say that benzodiazepines, such as Ativan, Xanax and Klonopin are effective for short-term stress, but that problems can arise when use continues for more than a few weeks. We knew it, Craig knew it, his doctors knew it. I remember when Craig was still a teenager and had been put on heavy-duty medications, including benzos, to combat his anxiety. We took him for a second opinion to a highly-recommended psychiatrist, who emphatically told us to get him off benzos. In stern language, he warned us that even low doses, over time, can cause seizures and long-term effects on the body and brain chemistry. Yet, over the years, Craig was often placed back on benzos, and once he became an adult, I was no longer part of the discussions he had with his doctors.

Craig Climbed a Tree

He tried to take his medications only as needed, but there were too many times when he needed them. He broke half milligrams into quarter milligrams when he felt that he could handle it. He complained about headaches, tingling, muscle twitches and "electric shocks," all side effects that medical literature attributes to both using benzos and withdrawing from them.

Then there were the antidepressants. High dosages left him both sleepy and unable to sleep, with stomach upset and other side effects. His complaints day-to-day sounded like we were dealing with a hypochondriac, not a young man in his twenties. We knew it, he knew it. He was "supposed" to tell his doctors what he was experiencing, and he tried to not be so drugged that he couldn't function. Over and over, he would ask us what to do. He suffered greatly, and we suffered greatly with him.

Craig loved music and especially folk. "Swimming to the Other Side," by Pat Humphries, was a favorite.

We are living 'neath the great Big Dipper
We are washed by the very same rain
We are swimming in the stream together
Some in power and some in pain
We can worship this ground we walk on
Cherishing the beings that we live beside

Fran and Craig Wishnick

Loving spirits will live forever
We're all swimming to the other side.

-Reprinted with permission

That song took on added, beautiful, and mournful meaning after July 27, 2011, the night our beloved child Craig ended his life by jumping off a bridge into the river waters. For us, it wasn't completely unexpected. A startling statement, perhaps, but we knew of his thoughts and desperation all too well. Craig ended his pain. He finally gave up hope that there was something better than his reality.

We are left with our indescribable memories. Profound loss, love, and knowing that he is with us, and changed us. We will never be the same.

It's been years now. My writing about him stopped, for months on end. I've wanted to write but couldn't; I have been emotional, my thoughts fuzzy and conflicted. Our inability to explain exactly what led to our son's final decision to end his life has been unnerving, and mixed with the deep sadness of his absence. Throughout Craig's life, his unique conglomeration of personal experiences, brain functions, and physical ailments were what I struggled to understand. Sometimes I tried way too hard. Other times I remember how I did not see a choice.

Craig Climbed a Tree

I have come around to this: I am unable to explain what pushed him over the edge. Craig's exhaustion and isolation, the medications streaming thru his slender body, his gastro-intestinal and immune system problems, and his experiences in life, the events with the hospital and systems of care, all meshed on that one day in a manner I'll never fully comprehend.

I have memories, heavy and hurting, troubling and contradictory. Memories of watching him try, in those last few months, on days when he wasn't bed-ridden. Trying to be in the world, while his options diminished. As his parents, we were totally spent. It's impossible to describe how little we had left to give to Craig, to anything. We tried to limit how much we told friends and family about his latest turns, because it was depressing to us, and we were exhausted from our efforts. Other people's attempts to focus on the positives did not reflect the reality of what was happening, and more than a few people turned away from us. We were simply too needy, and we knew it. He was isolated, and so were we.

We didn't know it was the end, but we knew that, once again, Craig was not doing well. We got a call that he had been hospitalized locally, after someone saw him walking on a bridge across the Hudson River, looking suspicious. He was hospitalized for about a week, and actually looked better in the middle of that week. When he was discharged, I noticed—and mentioned to the team—that he didn't look good. I was told he was highly medicated, and that his outpatient doctor would titrate his medication down. I asked Craig if he would like to stop at a favorite bakery, and he gobbled down some food -- in retrospect, in an animalistic type way I had never seen. I asked him if he wanted to come back to our house and stay, but he wanted to go back to his place.

He was an adult. We honored that. Ken stopped by and dropped off Craig's medications, but Craig didn't want to talk. Ken left.

Later that evening, the police came to our door. They had found Craig's ID under a bucket, at a spot where someone, apparently, had jumped. They were professional and kind. The police told us maybe it wasn't Craig, or maybe he had run away. I told them that I couldn't allow myself to hold out false hope. It was clear to us that Craig had actually taken his life.

Our boy. Our special son. He had ended it all. It was his 27th year.

He had made two phone calls. Both went to message. One was to his very special connection in Manhattan. He told Allie to be sure to remember to use animals to help other people like himself. The other call was to us: He told us he knew that we cared about him, but that he needed to do this.

He left a note:

It seems after being released from the hospital that the only way to feel comfortable in my own skin is to make a full-blown effort. I hope the effort ends positively because I'm sick of dealing with me (even though it's logical stuff.) Please remember to use these Trailways tickets – you have 8 tickets (4 roundtrips) to use by August 26th.

Epilogue

Today, there are apps for that. Apps for children who are easily frustrated, who have difficulty summarizing or prefer sequential information. Who are highly sensitive to sound and touch. There are apps for impulsivity, difficulty with conversations, and for concrete learners. Suicide prevention even has its own apps.

Craig was a generation removed from the app world. In addition to falling on the autism spectrum, he had a co-occurring mental health disorder, and almost lifelong suicidal ideations. But he was functional, apparently too functional for systems to wrap their services around him and help him. He could care for his basic needs, was medication compliant, and had strong executive functioning skills. On days when he felt well enough, he could and did plan out his day, making his way around the

New York City subway system and attending conferences on his many interest areas.

He just couldn't figure out how to survive, and the systems designed to help people couldn't help him. He didn't fit their boxes (in current jargon, silos). He had serious and persistent mental illness, and was somewhere on the autism spectrum. Most importantly, he had enormous strengths. Those strengths actually worked against him.

Craig scored quite high on the New York State Professional Careers Test. 100% on quantitative analysis, and 84% on understanding and interpreting written material (related to government and social issues). He wanted to work; he needed to work, to feel connected to the world and not helpless. Yet employment had to be part-time, around his health and mental health needs, and customized to his abilities and disabilities. That particular person-centered help was unavailable to him.

A classification as developmentally disabled would have opened opportunities for customized employment that were unavailable to him, because he was too functional.

The New York State Office of Mental Health says that "caring for someone with disclosed risk of suicide requires knowledge and skills to manage risk appropriately."

Yet Craig didn't qualify for the ACT (Assertive Community Treatment) program because he was medication compliant and, again, too functional. Unless he was actively suicidal, he was left on his own in an outpatient world trying to live. If he hospitalized himself too often, he was reprimanded. In hospitals settings, as soon as his acute phase was deemed to be over, he was discharged. He could not access a Partial Hospitalization Program because he wouldn't sign a Contract for Safety, even though contracts for safety have been proven to be an unacceptable tool in suicide prevention. For all practical purposes, Craig was isolated and on his own, and so were we as his family.

When Craig was discharged from his last psychiatric hospitalization, he was scheduled for his next outpatient appointment. There was no follow-up, no circling of the wagons, even though he was at high-risk. For him, it was a never-ending cycle without the help that he needed, specific to him as a person, with his unique strengths and disabilities.

There is a need for massive system change.

Craig ended his cycle of despair. We remember when he climbed the tree.

Craig Climbed a Tree

ACKNOWLEDGEMENTS

Craig Climbed a Tree took almost five years to write. I am grateful to amazing friends – old, new and very new - for understanding the power of Craig's words and experiences. They listened, read the pages, encouraged and critiqued, while also helping me to continue processing my immense grief. They discerned my intent and need to get this vital book published, thereby helping many people over time.

My deepest thanks of appreciation to:
Donna Weintraub, Michael Seereiter, Mike Hogan, Allison Kleinman, Wanda Fischer, Joan Lawrence-Bauer, Denise Ranaghan, Deb Schultz, Mira Bowin, Marsha Lazarus, Sue Hoger, Lindsay Miller, Susan Dooha and my friends at NYS Independent Living Centers, Nancy Cohen, Karen Sherwood, Ellen Pendegar and my fellow board members at the Mental Health Association in Ulster, Barb Horneff, Linda Breithaupt, Ruth Quinn, Christopher Duncan, Ellen Rocco, Susan Wortas, Robin Taliaferro, Charlene Dye, Renee Fillette, Ellen Riojas Clark, Susan Slotnick David Shepler, Gavin de Becker and Caroline Paulson.

Craig Climbed a Tree

I am grateful to Kathy Ness and Connie Happeny who came into our lives through Craig's second dog, Theo.

Most new friends never met Craig but grew to know him through this book. In itself, that fulfills part of the book's purpose.

Thanks to my aunt, Bobbie Simon and cousin, Marcia Wizelman who read each chapter in the initial stages and encouraged me to continue. I am grateful to Pat Humphries for permission to include part of her song, "Swimming to the Other Side."

Appreciation to Greg Correll of Small Packages and Design for his compassionate understanding, his expert eye and suggestions to make the book read well and his beautiful cover artwork and book design.

Finally, utmost thanks to my husband Ken for listening, over and over, as I read the book out loud and for hearing all my writer's angst while he worked through his own emotions. Ken's full support in all ways made this book possible.

Fran Wishnick

Made in the USA
San Bernardino, CA
16 April 2017